Collins

need to know?

Buying Property in France

Penny Zoldan

Collins

First published in 2006 by Collins
an imprint of
HarperCollins Publishers
77–85 Fulham Palace Road
London W6 8JB

www.collins.co.uk

10 09 08 07 06
6 5 4 3 2 1

© HarperCollins Publishers, 2006

All rights reserved. No part of this publication
may be reproduced, stored in a retrieval system,
or transmitted, in any form or by any means,
electronic, mechanical, photocopying, recording
or otherwise, without the prior written permission
of the publishers.

A catalogue record for this book is available from
the British Library

Penny Zoldan asserts the moral right to be identified
as the author of this work.

Editor: Heather Thomas
Design: Rolando Ugolini
Photographs: All photographs provided by Latitudes
except for the following by Trevor Yorke: pages 30,
42, 62, 76, 88, 104, 120, 135, 144, 147, 150, 162, 175,
179, 180 and 183
Front cover photograph: © Owen Franken/Corbis
Back cover photographs: Latitudes

ISBN-13 978 0 00 720777 0
ISBN-10 0 00 720777 8

Colour reproduction by Colourscan, Singapore
Printed and bound by Printing Express Ltd,
Hong Kong

Contents

Why France?

For most people, the decision to buy in France will come easily. They have become Francophiles without even noticing, and love France and all things French. They want to enjoy the ambience and *joie de vivre* of the French lifestyle.

The French seem to know how to enjoy life and they appreciate the finer things it has to offer without letting little daily aggravations get in the way. In France at lunchtime, for instance, everything and everyone stops, from builders and managers to office workers and farmers.

Most areas of France offer something to do at all times of the year and in all weathers – there are lots of festivals and shows, and indoor and outdoor activities and sports. This choice of leisure pursuits is another reason why people choose France over many other European destinations, where the British buy homes just to live in the sun in an ex-pat community. Most communes have public tennis courts and swimming pools and many offer facilities for children's activities throughout the holidays. In France you can become involved in the day-to-day life of a village or town and feel part of it but at the same time have friends of your own nationality.

If you want to immerse yourself totally into France and French culture, then choose your areas carefully so that you find yourself with like-minded people with some common interests. For instance, if you are a born-and-bred townie then it may be that you would not have much to say in the local bar to the farmers who know only a simple rural life. Even though the idea of a less stressful lifestyle is appealing, you may still be looking for some entertaining conversation.

You will be buying in France because you want to. So try to enjoy the process, the decisions, the search and the purchase – use your common sense. Only deal with the estate agencies with whom you feel most comfortable or which have been recommended specifically to you. You should handle the process as they do in France; do not expect it to be the same as the procedure in the UK.

Above all, don't panic! Buying property is generally a good investment, and should you find that once you have your property you are not as happy with it as you thought, you can always resell it and start again. You are more likely to make a profit than a loss, unlike most other purchases, however big or small, especially cars. Indeed, these can be more irreversible decisions because as soon as you buy a car, it decreases in value. However, your property should increase or at least hold its value. The longer you own it the more likely it is that you will make a good capital gain. This book will help guide you through the process of buying your dream home in France.

1 How to get started

Before you begin your search for a property in France in earnest there are various decisions that you will need to make, such as where you want to live, the size of your budget, your timescale, and the size and type of property you require. Read through the following pages and learn how to get started.

Where to look

The three most important things to consider when buying a property are location, location and location – everything else about the property can be changed – albeit at a cost.

must know

Getting there
If you are planning to use your French home at regular intervals make sure your journey is easy and pleasant or you will find that when the novelty wears off you will use the property less. Invest in a map of France so you can view the whole country and get some idea of the relationship of one area to another. Also buy a map book (1 cm = 2 km) so that you can look up towns and villages. Bear in mind that you will need to allow one hour to cover 100 km (62 miles) on a motorway and one hour to cover 50 km (30 miles) on normal roads in normal circumstances.

Which area?

It may be that you are not too concerned about where you buy your property but are more particular about what you purchase and how much it costs. Bear in mind, though, that France is a huge country (two-and-a-half times the size of the UK) and if you are physically going to be able to view a selection of properties then you will need to limit the areas so that they will be within a reasonable distance of each other. Therefore you will need to come to a decision as to where you want to look before you start your serious viewing. To help you decide, consider the following and then visit the areas that you feel would suit you best.

Climate

Many people move abroad to get more sunshine. Research all the areas that you are interested in carefully – all areas of France have some cold weather but the further south you go, the longer and warmer the summers. So if guaranteed hot and sunny summers filled with barbecues and warm evening sundowners are what you have in mind then make sure to look at least south of the Loire Valley. The French tourist office in London is a good source of information about the weather. You can also search on the Internet for further details about the climate in specific areas.

Accessibility

For any area that interests you, check its proximity to both national and regional airports and the regularity of flights to the UK airports that are nearest to your home. This is particularly important if you plan to visit on a regular basis, and if you expect to have lots of visitors. Find out whether the nearest railway station has a TGV service, and look into motorway access and ferry services. France has an excellent network of motorways, which all lead to and from Paris. Research the costs of your journey carefully.

Flights

There are flights to Paris from most UK airports and from there connections to most French cities both by plane and train. Nice is a particularly well served airport with more than a dozen flights a day from all London airports and several other UK airports, while Languedoc Roussillon has a choice of four airports to fly into. Increasingly, there are more direct flights from the UK to smaller

Proximity to facilities

You might want to think about buying a property near to one or more of the following:
- Golf courses
- Fishing lakes
- Tennis courts and indoor centres
- Horse riding centres
- Canoeing and boating centres
- Ski slopes
- Country or mountain walks
- Cycle lanes
- Children's activities
- Seaside and water sports
- Marinas and moorings
- Shops and boutiques – not just essential supplies
- Restaurants and bars

Property exhibitions are a good way of collecting information on the French property market.

must know

Local services
In areas of France that are remote it is usual that bread deliveries are made daily and there are often travelling shops with everyday supplies. School buses provide transport for students of all ages if schools are not within walking distance.

airports in France, so in most French towns and cities you are likely to have a choice of airports within close proximity to give you more flexibility. And if all else fails, i.e. flights or trains are cancelled, you can always drive home if you have to return urgently – this will make you feel more comfortable if you are intending leaving family or friends for any length of time. Rural locations in central France, which are well away from large towns, are unlikely to be close to airports, main stations or motorways so they will take longer to reach – something that will appeal to a great number of people who really want to get away from it all.

Public transport

If you don't drive, then you will also need to check on public transport. Buses are not available in many less populated and rural locations. Although the larger towns will have some sort of service it can be difficult to get from one town or village to another – having a car and being able to drive is essential in some areas. However, you may find that a bicycle allows you to get to some means of transport if you really don't want to drive.

Amenities and activities

If you are buying a property for use either as a second home or holiday home, you will be doing so for your enjoyment. So think carefully about how you would like to spend your time when you are in France – your hobbies, leisure activities and pastimes. If you are looking for a main residence, then you will have to research your area even more carefully as you will need to think about jobs and schools. A good way to proceed is to make a list and then take advice from an agent who covers most of France to find out which area offers as many as possible of the requirements on your list.

Thanks to improved transport systems and budget airlines, a villa with a pool in southern France is now easily accessible.

Régions and départements

France is divided into *régions* and then *départements* of which there are 95, numbered in alphabetical order. The post code will tell you immediately which area a given place is in – car number plates always have this number last to indicate where the car is registered.

must know

Council offices
Depending on the size of village and towns, these will be situated in the *Hôtel de Ville* or the *Mairie*.

Numbers and post codes

The major town in a *département* is where the *préfecture* is based and this is usually indicated by its post code – the *département* number followed by 000 – so, for instance, the postcode for Nice is 06000. When hiring a car there are certain *département* numbers that are most often used, e.g. 60, so be aware that your car will stand out as a hired car and therefore could be a target for theft if the locals believe you are a tourist and may have valuables inside.

Régions in France

Nord Pas de Calais
Pas de Calais 62
Nord 59

Picardie
Somme 80
Oise 60
Aisne 02

Haute Normandie
Seine Maritime 76
Eure 27

Basse Normandie
Manche 50
Calvados 14
Orne 61

Bretagne
Finistère 29
Côtes d'Armor 22
Morbihan 56
Ille et Vilaine 35

Ile de France
Paris 75
Seine et Marne 77
Yvelines 78

Essonne 91
Hauts de Seine 92
Seine Saint Denis 93
Val de Marne 94
Val d'Oise 95

Champagne Ardenne
Ardennes 08
Marne 51
Haute Marne 52
Aube 10

Lorraine
Meuse 55
Moselle 57
Meurthe et Moselle 54
Vosges 88

Alsace
Bas Rhin 67
Haut Rhin 68

Pays de la Loire
Loire Atlantique 44
Mayenne 53
Sarthe 72
Maine et Loire 49
Vendée 85

Centre
Eure et Loir 28
Indre et Loire 37
Loir et Cher 41
Loiret 45
Indre 36
Cher 18

Bourgogne
Yonne 89
Nièvre 58
Côte d'Or 21
Saône et Loire 71

Franche Comté
Haute Saône 70
Doubs 25
Jura 39
Térritoire de Belfort 90

Poitou Charente
Deux Sèvres 79
Vienne 86
Charente 16
Charente Maritime 17

Limousin
Haute Vienne 87

Nord Pas
de Calais

62 59

76
80

Haute
Normandie
50

02 08
Picardie

60
14 27

95 77
78

Ile de
France

91

45 89

51 55

57
67

Lorraine
54

88

Alsace

68

Basse
Normandie
61
29 22
Bretagne
56
35 53
72

Pays de
la Loire
44 49
37
41
Centre
18

Champagne
Ardenne
10

52
70
90
25
21

58

Bourgogne

71

Franche
Comté
39

85 79
86
36
03

28

Poitou
Charente
17 16
87 23
Limousin
19
63
42
38
01 74
Rhône Alpes
73

24
Auvergne
15 43

07
05

33
47
46
Midi
Pyrénées
82
81
12
48
26
30
84
Provence
04

Côte
d'Azur
06

Aquitaine
40 32
34
13
83

64

65
31
09
11

Languedoc
Roussillon

66

Corse 28

2A

Régions in France *continued*

Creuse 23
Corrèze 19

Auvergne
Allier 03
Puy de Dôme 63
Cantal 15
Haute Loire 43

Aquitaine
Gironde 33
Dordogne 24
Landes 40
Lot et Garonne 47
Pyrénées Atlantiques 64

Rhône Alpes
Loire 42
Rhône 69
Ain 01
Savoie 73
Haute Savoie 74
Isère 38
Drôme 26
Ardèche 07

Midi Pyrénées
Lot 46
Aveyron 12
Tarn et Garonne 82
Tarn 81

Gers 32
Haute Garonne 31
Hautes Pyrénées 65
Ariège 09

**Languedoc
Roussillon**
Lozère 48
Gard 30
Hérault 34
Aude 11
Pyrénées Orientales 66

Provence
Hautes Alpes 05

Alpes de Haute
Provence 04
Vaucluse 84
Bouches du Rhône 13
Var 83

Côte d'Azur
Alpes Maritimes 06

Corse
Haute Corse 2B
Corse du Sud 2A

Work out what you want

Are you buying to get away from it all, or do you love shopping and sitting in cafés watching the world go by? Is going out to eat and having a vast choice of good restaurants high on your list or will you be happy with one or two local restaurants?

must know

Location
Check out that the property not only has a view but has the right orientation for the sun so that you can sit on your terrace and enjoy it.

Urban or rural life?

Do you want to be close to a major town with sophisticated and comprehensive stores or will village shops suffice? If you want to buy a rural property, consider whether you really want to be totally isolated or would prefer to be near other houses.

Don't expect to find a property offering you proximity to all the sporting and leisure activities in a rural and sparsely populated part of France – amenities are for people and will be found in areas of higher population or tourist areas. Nor should you assume that an area is overrun with Brits just because you know a lot of people holiday there – there is a huge difference in the number of people who spend holidays in any area to those who own homes there. It is always a good idea to look at any area you are interested in out of season. To get good value from your property in France you will want to use it throughout the year, so make sure there is lots to interest you in the local area in the depths of winter as well as the height of summer.

Scenery

If a view is really important to you, remember that it is often the reason that one property is more expensive than its neighbour. Sea views command particularly high prices, followed by mountains and rolling countryside, so you will have to do a balancing act between your ideal property and ideal budget. If you insist on a sea view, remember that it can almost double the price in some areas. Open country views can make a property with a small garden feel spacious and can be well worth the extra cost for the feeling of space they impart. Distant snow-capped mountain views can be pleasing when you are sitting in the sunshine, but you may have to move further away from amenities and neighbours than you would wish in order to get a panoramic view – the decision is yours, but compromises on your ideal will always have to be made. A prettily planted garden can be just as pleasing to wake up to.

Budget

One of the most important decisions that you will have to make is the amount of money you are prepared or able to invest in your French property. Before you embark on purchasing a property in France, make sure you understand the costs that are involved. If you are going to buy with a mortgage, check with a broker or French bank as to how much they will be prepared to offer you.

Check out the price

In most cases, the prices quoted include the agency's commission but not the *notaire*'s fees and taxes – which are the equivalent of the UK solicitor's fees and stamp duty. Always check with your agent as to what their quoted price includes, as some agencies in France will not include their charges unlike most agents in the UK who sell properties in France. UK-based agencies normally work on a shared commission with their French partner agency so that the total cost will be exactly the same as if you went direct to the local French agency – again, check this out in advance. If a UK agency wants to make any extra charges then find another one. The role of these agents differs from agents selling UK properties and is much more comprehensive. You can also buy through some *notaires* and again you need to check what is included in their price.

Prices can vary

As a guide, property prices are higher near to the coast, the lakes and close to or in the major towns and cities. Particularly expensive spots are the Côte d'Azur, the Lubéron and around Aix-en-Provence, Paris, Biarritz, Annécy and top-class alpine resorts, such as Courchevel, Mégève and

Consider carefully the type of property you wish to buy. It could be in a rural or secluded location, or close to a wide range of amenities and the hustle and bustle of a village or town.

Chamonix to name but a few. Properties in central and rural France are cheaper. Proximity to airports offering flights to major European and worldwide destinations increases the price.

Obviously prices are higher in more popular regions but take account of the fact that the popularity is normally justified due to the benefits offered in those areas. For instance, the Côte d'Azur is one of the most attractive coastlines in the world and has the best weather in France, thanks to its micro-climate. Tourist attractions such as the caves and the river in the Dordogne, the bastide towns with wonderful views in the Vaucluse, ski resorts with their limited areas and therefore limited property availability, and the gorges and pretty villages in the Tarn et Garonne, Languedoc and Aveyron, combined with reasonable proximity to major towns and airports, all contribute to higher prices. But remember also that a property which is located in an area that is in demand is more likely to increase in value than one in a less popular area.

Ongoing costs and utilities

The ongoing costs of owning a property, including utility bills, maintenance and travel, need to be budgeted for, but against this take account of the savings you will make on holiday accommodation for you and your family and possibly friends too, which may well be greater than the annual costs.

When you are looking at properties you can ask their vendors to give you some idea of the charges for utilities, and in some cases they may be able to show you bills. But if they are full-time owners and you want a holiday home you will have to take account of how much less energy you will use and remember that the cost will depend on the tariff that you decide to take. Remember also that if you are going to use your property more during the summer months, then your heating bills will be negligible, and even if you are using it in the winter months and leaving your home in the UK you will probably save more than it would cost at home as the weather is not so cold in many areas of France.

Renting out your property

If you would like to mitigate your costs or make money from your property, you might think about renting it out, either commercially or just to friends to help with the running costs and the repayment of your mortgage, if you have one. You can rent through a French rental agency, a UK rental agency, normally just for holiday lets, through magazine advertising or just word of mouth to friends and friends of friends. You can rent out for all, most or just some of the time – perhaps only a few weeks a year. If you choose to let the property in high season, just a few weeks may cover the running costs, and a couple of months or more may pay your mortgage. In effect, this makes the use of your property free to you by getting others to pay off your loan.

Mortgages

Why not look into the possibility of taking out a mortgage on a house in France? This could be the route to achieving your dream home or it may allow you to buy a house in good order rather than a run-down one at a knock-down price which needs a considerable amount of work and money lavished on it to make it habitable.

The time scale

The purchase procedure in France works to a different time scale to that in the UK and you need to be aware of it in order to plan your timing to purchase. In France you will be expected to sign the first contract (*compromis*) almost immediately the sale price is agreed.

must know

Paying a deposit
On signing the first contract you will normally be expected to pay a 10 per cent deposit – although sometimes five per cent is possible. For new properties this is the norm, but it could be as low as two per cent. It will depend on the developer and the timescale allowed for the construction. Be mindful that the contract can be subject to getting a mortgage – in fact, you cannot put in your full mortgage application without sending a copy of a signed contract.

Time is of the essence

You could visit a property at 10 am and then sign the *compromis* before lunch. The purchase procedure will be dealt with in detail later in this book, but normally it takes a minimum of two months before the signing of the final *acte*, i.e. completion of the property. It can be longer if both the purchaser and the vendor would like it to be, and it is normally longer when you are buying a new property, which is bought off-plan.

Conditions

The sale may have other conditions included but it is not normally acceptable for it to be subject to the sale of your property in the UK or elsewhere as the timing on this is not quantifiable and the vendor of the French property could be left waiting with a fixed priced contract to sell for many months or longer. If you have a property to sell but want to proceed with a purchase nevertheless, you need a mortgage on the French property in the meantime.

It is sometimes possible to get a vendor to agree a sale which is subject to the sale of your property if it is already in a solicitor's hands in the UK – if so, it will have a time limit on it so if the UK sale does not proceed, the French contract will become null and void and your deposit will be returned by the *notaire*.

Buying a second home

Bearing all this in mind, many people decide to wait until their property is sold before going to view in France. If you are buying a second home you are probably just downsizing – so you will be looking in the UK at the same time. Moving is stressful at the best of times, so it is advisable to get yourself settled first and then start househunting in France – after all, it should be an enjoyable experience, not a hassle.

Making a permanent move

This may mean that you need to arrange rental accommodation in the UK or France after you have sold your property and whilst you look in France, but it is certainly preferable to finding the property of your dreams and then not being able to proceed because you are restricted by not having sold your UK property, which is extremely frustrating. However, if you decide to rent in France, then try to organize the timing so that you are not in high season as this could be expensive – if you need to rent out of season it will be relatively cheap.

Don't expect to feel the same as you will in your own home if you decide to rent in France – it really will be different. Your neighbours may not go to the same trouble to get to know you and help you to settle in; and you will not have time to get to know the villagers as you will be constantly searching for properties and never really feeling settled. However, don't let this put you off making the permanent move – in many cases, it might be better to rent in the UK whilst you look as you may feel more comfortable about making decisions on your own familiar territory.

must know

How many trips?
Remember that the cost of every exploratory trip can add up – flights, hire car, hotel, meals – so if your budget is tight, once you have decided on the area and checked out the properties, try to keep your trips to a minimum and put the money towards the property instead. As properties can be sold, i.e. contracts signed, within minutes of a client visiting, it is impossible for any agency to be 100 per cent certain that a property will be available by the time you are able to see it.

Be prepared

Even if you are not quite ready to proceed with purchasing a house in France, it is perfectly sensible to contact some agents and collect property details and information on different areas so that you have a good idea of what you will be able to purchase with the money you have available and can be more realistic about potential properties when you are ready to start house-hunting in earnest.

However, do be honest with your estate agent about your time scale. Any agent will be happy to send you a list of suitable properties so that you get some idea of what to expect for your money, but there is no point having more and more sent until you are ready to make a selection and to go to France to start viewing them. You can also use this time to prepare yourself – to explore what different areas have to offer and look out for bargain flight offers perhaps so that you can make a few trips to the areas you think might be of interest.

Explore the area

It may also be worth making a viewing trip to the area of your choice if only to make sure that you will be able to find something to suit you rather than have unrealistic expectations – but do make sure that you tell your agent that at this stage you are just looking. You don't want the agency to give up on you before you are ready to proceed when you will really need their help.

Eating a delicious lunch with family and friends on the sunny terrace of your new French home could soon become a reality.

must know

Websites
These can be extremely useful when you are researching property prices. They can help you to select areas that you can afford and also to see what architectural styles, condition and size of properties are available. However, make sure that the websites you search are updated frequently and that the properties are available to avoid any disappointment.

Size and type of property

The size of the property you end up buying will depend on your budget to a certain extent, but there are several decisions you need to make. Do you want it to be ready to move into? And are you prepared to do some work or major renovations?

must know

Property descriptions

Agents in France prepare much briefer details than is the norm in the UK. They are not governed by such strict rules as to their descriptions and UK agents can only pass on what they are given.

How much work?

There are many properties in France, especially in rural areas, that are described as being habitable but which most of us would not want to live in. Decorating and replacing kitchens and bathrooms are not considered to be renovation, so do make sure that your agent understands how much work you are prepared to do on a property or you may end up wasting your time viewing totally unsuitable ones.

Architectural styles

These will vary from area to area so check that what you have set your heart on, whether it's a stone property or a *colombage* (traditional Normandy farmhouse), is available in the region you have chosen. For instance, stone properties are found in those areas where stone was mined so there's no point looking for them in other areas. There are specific names for different types of properties in particular areas of France.

▶ A *mas* is a rectangular stone property found in the south; it is simply built with smallish windows to keep out the sun.

▶ A *bastide* is similarly built of stone but it is a little more imposing and normally double fronted.

▶ A *maison de maître* – literally, a master's house – is a double-fronted reasonably imposing property, which is usually in a town and dates from the nineteenth century.

▶ A *longère* is a long, low property, a term more often used in northern France.

▶ A *fermette* is a small farmhouse, normally in northern France.

Climate considerations

You should always take account of the climate when you are thinking about the size of the property you want to purchase in France. If you want to live in the warmer regions in the south of the country, then the outside space, be it a balcony, terrace or garden, is going to be a priority for you. For 60 or 70 per cent of the year, your outside areas will be an important part of your living space while the interior space will be far less important.

The direction in which the property faces is another consideration when you are house-hunting. A south-facing house will catch lots of sun throughout the day, but remember also that in hot climates north-facing rooms can be beneficial as they stay cool in the intense heat of summer.

Each area has its own architectural styles, so make sure that the sort of property you are looking for is available in the area you have chosen. This Provençal stone house is typical of the region with its small windows, cool interior and covered terrace.

This *colombage manoir* in Normandy is typical of the style of traditional timber-framed farmhouses in this region.

Extensions and conversions

In France the size of property that you can build on a piece of land is normally regulated and you can check at the local *Mairie* (town hall) as to whether the property you have seen is built to the maximum size allowed or whether you would be allowed to extend it. Your agent will be able to check at the *Mairie* and advise you on this once you have viewed the property and have decided that you could be interested in purchasing it.

If the property in which you are interested has outbuildings that are not living accommodation, you will need to apply for a *certificat d'urbanisme* – an application to confirm whether, subject to planning permission, you can turn the outbuilding into living accommodation. If the outbuildings are attached to the main house, permission is much easier to obtain; if not, it can take some months. However, the agent will do this for you and it can be a condition of your contract if the vendor agrees to this, so if you are refused you will get your deposit back.

Make sure you have accounted within your budget for any work you are going to take on, such as converting existing outbuildings – it can sometimes be cheaper to buy something that already has what you need rather than taking on the responsibility of additional work and, perhaps, escalating costs.

Size

Make a comprehensive list of everything you would like your property to have, such as a large garden, four bedrooms, countryside location, etc. Your agent can be most helpful if they have a list of what you consider most important, with your minimum requirements and maximum budget.

Measurements are always in metres – and usually given in square metres, i.e. rooms of 12 m², 15 m² or 30 m² rather than 15 x 3 m. In most cases the agency will not have taken the measurements in any other way and thus they cannot give full room measurements.

The outbuildings that come with this house could be converted into *gîtes*, but check that you can get permission to do the conversion before signing a contract.

In southern France where the
summers are hotter and longer,
it is important to have a terrace
and outdoor living space.

The overall habitable surface of the property will be given in square metres, as will the surface area of the land. Whereas we talk about a property having two, three or four bedrooms, a French agent will say a property is a two, three, four or five 'piece-property' – i.e. how many rooms it has not including the kitchen and bathrooms. If you are asked what size property you require, an answer is expected in square metres, i.e. 100m².

It is a good idea to measure one or two rooms in your own house and then put them into square metres to give yourself a better idea of room sizes as you may be more accustomed to thinking in feet and inches. Remember there are 39 inches in a metre; and 4000 m² is one acre.

Utilities

Utilities are charged differently but the overall cost is not dissimilar, obviously depending on how much time you spend at the property and in which season. Water is always metered, heating can be electric, town gas, *gaz* (in a canister or tank) or oil. Some boilers can be oil or wood burning and even use corn cobs for fuel. There are various tariffs for fuel from which you can choose, and you will need to discuss these with your local office to determine which would work out best for you for the periods of time that you will be using the property.

The French utility companies are accommodating to second-home owners and will happily send the bills to the UK a couple of weeks before payment is due and then take the payment from your French bank account by direct debit on the due date. This will give you time to make sure that the money is in your account. Remember that you will need to open a bank account in France if you own a property there and this will be covered later on in the book.

want to know more?

Take it to the next level...

▶ Renting 56
▶ Getting a mortgage 78, 108
▶ Extensions and conversions 55
▶ Utilities 142, 148

Other sources...

▶ *Vive la France* exhibition is held at Olympia in London each January: www.vivelafrance.co.uk
▶ For details of French property exhibitions around the UK, see: www.french-property-news.com
▶ For information on French regions, amenities and travel, contact the French Tourist Office (see page 188) or see: www.francetourism.com
▶ To obtain local information on specific areas, go to: www.pocket.angloinfo.com
▶ For weather information: www.meteofrance.com
▶ Buy Michelin map No. 721, the best folding map of all France, plus individual maps of the area you have chosen to look in.

2 How to find property in France

There is no substitute for going to France to see a range of properties, and your first viewing trip is bound to be a huge learning curve – a real education. You will begin to understand what is meant by the brief details you have received on various interesting properties, and you will also gain a much better insight into the French property market and how the system works in practice.

Where to look

So how do you start looking for your dream home? There are lots of starting points to help you, ranging from property exhibitions in the UK to magazines, internet sites and estate agents.

Exhibitions

Several French property exhibitions are held every year in the UK which will offer you the opportunity of talking to agencies, both UK- and French-based companies, without any obligation. Although there are many overseas property exhibitions which cover most countries, if you have definitely decided on France then it is more practical to visit the French-only exhibitions where there will be a greater choice of agencies and subsidiary services regarding purchasing in France.

French property exhibitions will help you choose areas that interest you and enable you to discuss your requirements with experienced agents based in the UK and in France.

Vive la France is the major exhibition in the UK – this is especially useful as it has not only the biggest array of agencies but also tourist office stands for gathering information and discussing different regions. This gives you the opportunity to talk to people who live and work in the areas that interest you.

As well as London, specialist French property exhibitions are held throughout the year in towns and cities such as Birmingham, Harrogate, Dublin and Taunton, all of which only feature French property and related services, such as solicitors, currency exchange and removal companies.

However, if you have already decided where you want to buy in France, you might find that your time and money are better spent on making a reconnaissance trip to that area in order to start viewing properties, having contacted some agents in advance to arrange appointments for you.

Websites

As mentioned earlier, property websites are a great source of information for finding out what you can get for your budget in a particular area and for seeing the type and architecture of properties that are generally available there. See the directory at the end of this book (page 188) for a list of recommended sites. There are also websites for general regional information and even for some smaller towns as well as the latest information on the weather and events.

Magazines

Magazines specializing in French property can also be helpful when you are looking for a home. They feature useful information about areas, events, properties coming onto the market, letters from like-minded people and, often, case studies on Francophiles who have already made the move, as well as a vast array of agents' advertisements. Some of these magazines, such as *Living France, France, Everything France and French*, can be bought in newsagents, whereas others can be mailed direct to you.

Estate agencies

You should contact agents for property information and listings. You will soon discover that estate agencies dealing with France work in a very different way to a local UK agency.

must know

Property descriptions
Do not expect to find the same level of detail in property descriptions prepared by French agencies – they often only give the square meterage, not room measurements; nor do they give the exact location, just a close one. The reason for this is that they feel that it is always going to be factors such as ambience, position and outlook that will enable you to make a decision, so you will need to view any property that interests you. The French accept this, so bear in mind that when in France you need to accept the way they do things. The help and assistance you will receive when you meet with them will make up for the lack of advance information.

Most people looking for a property in France will end up dealing with a French estate agent.

Which agency?

You have the choice of either dealing with agencies that are based in France or agencies based in the UK which deal with French property, albeit normally in association with a French agent (*agent immobilier*).

French-based French agencies

To own an estate agency in France, you must have a *carte professionnelle* and to obtain this you must have 10 years' experience of working in an agency or a law degree. Each agency must be registered with the local town hall, hold a *carte professionnelle* and have a bank guarantee. You will often see a certificate hanging on an agency's walls confirming this, and you are at liberty at any time to ask to see their *carte professionnelle* number – don't be afraid to ask if they have one and also to see details of their charges.

Without a *carte professionnelle*, an estate agent does not have the right to hold a 'mandate' to sell a property or to take clients to view properties. It is a necessity, and should there be any queries, any questions you need answered, or problems with your purchase, only a registered agent will be in a position to sort these things out for you. Do not be tempted by someone offering to show you a few properties that 'friends' have for sale – if they are acting as an agent and do not hold a *carte professionnelle*, they are acting illegally.

Bear in mind that French estate agents are not used to sending out property descriptions by post as we have come to expect in the UK, so do not hold your breath if you have phoned or emailed to ask for details – they might never arrive. Also, French agencies have to accompany their clients to view properties; they can't just send them along or give them a set of keys.

FNAIM

This is a similar organization in France to the NAEA (National Association of Estate Agents) in the UK. It is a regulatory body and although it is not essential that an estate agent is a member, it is an additional comfort for a buyer to know that their agent is a member of a regulatory body.

The specialist French property exhibitions, such as *Vive la France*, are now extremely popular.

Agency fees

A fixed list (*barème*) of an agency's commission is often displayed on the wall of their office. Agency fees in France are higher than those in the UK as their role differs greatly (as will be explained later). You can expect the agency fees to amount to between five and ten per cent of the purchase price of a property; normally, the higher the price the lower the percentage charged. This percentage includes TVA (VAT) at 19.6 per cent which the agent has to pay to the authorities. The total amount is normally included in the quoted price, but do check!

Sole, multiple and shared agencies

French agencies have to have a signed mandate to sell each property they carry on their books. Each vendor giving an agency a property to sell will be asked to sign a document confirming their instructions to sell, the price and the commission, etc. In some cases the agents may have a sole agency, i.e. no other agent is instructed – it is a good idea to ask about this if you see a property you like and need some thinking time. If other estate agencies have been instructed they could be showing their clients the property and your agent will have no idea that they are proceeding until informed that it has been sold. It is quite usual for French agencies to share their properties with other local agencies to give you a wider choice. They will then share the commission, and it will not cost you any more.

Purchasing procedure

French agents are permitted to draw up the first contract (*compromis*) and hold deposits in their client's account. If you require further information on a specific property that you are prepared to purchase with regard to extending or changing it in any way, the agent will go to the *Mairie* (town hall) for you or with you to find out the possibilities.

During the purchase procedure, the agent will liaise between you and the *notaire* if you wish and is always in attendance at the *notaire's* office for the final signing and transfer of the property – sometimes even acting in the capacity of translator. Bear in mind that the agent is based close to your property and they probably live nearby and have done so all their life – they

must know

Local knowledge
Most French agencies deal with their local area, which may cover a radius of as much as 100 km (63 miles). Their knowledge is second to none and they are extremely proud of their region and will act as tourist guides whilst they are showing you around. You can learn a lot about the region, weather, activities, accessibility, house prices, schools, hospitals and other facilities. In fact, in the space of a morning's viewing you can often gain more knowledge than in several days' research at home in the UK.

have a reputation to uphold and can fill you in on all the information you need on the area. They will want to make sure that you are pleased with their service as there is every likelihood that they will be bumping into you in the future at the local shops and restaurants – estate agents are respected members of society in France. Some French agents employ British staff, which can be very useful as they can give you information regarding making the move and buying as a foreigner, etc. However, do check that they are working legally for the agency.

UK-based French agents

The role of an agent based in the UK and dealing solely with French property is to smooth the way for prospective purchasers. These agents will normally work in partnership with French-based agencies, and whereas some will specialize in a certain area of France, others will cover most of the areas. They may be members of regulatory bodies such as FOPDAC and NAEA and will have to have proved themselves to be members of these associations

The advantage of dealing with an agent who is based in the UK and covers most of France is that they can give you a good overview of the differences between areas, i.e. house prices, types of property, weather and accessibility. When you are trying to decide between different areas, this information can be extremely helpful, plus the fact that they can send you details of comparably priced properties in the areas you are considering. They will also be able to advise you on journey times from one area to another as they will be accustomed to travelling in France on a regular basis.

Pros and cons of French versus English agents

French agents

Pros

- They know their areas inside out.
- They know each of their properties.
- They will accompany you to each property.
- If working with a UK agent, they will be prepared for the extra work involved dealing with UK purchasers.
- They work on an appointment basis.
- They can tell you what price they think the vendor might take whereas in the UK they are not allowed to do this.

Cons

- They are probably limited to one area.
- There may be a language problem.
- If they are unaccustomed to dealing with UK purchasers they may not be prepared to assist with problems outside of the sale, i.e. utilities, planning, etc.
- They may not have a full understanding of UK purchasers' expectations.
- They do not send out details to purchasers as a matter of course.

UK-based French property agents

Pros

- They can give you a better overview of various areas.
- They will arrange a viewing itinerary covering several agencies and possibly several areas.
- They will have a better understanding of your requirements and expectations and can ask questions for you.
- They will be able to explain the purchase procedure and assist all the way through it together with their French associates.
- They should be fluent in French and can assist your dealings with the French agent and *notaire*.

Cons

- They will not have seen each property individually.
- They are not allowed to take you to view properties in France unless they have a *carte professionnelle*.
- Properties could be sold between the time it takes to make viewing appointments and travel to France to see them.
- Many new agents are being set up, but as they do not have to register in the UK, you should check out their background and history.

As well as having valuable local knowledge about a range of areas, they will be in a position to make appointments for you with long-established and very knowledgeable French agencies which have been vetted by the UK company. These will be agents who have elected to work with the UK market, who enjoy doing so and are prepared for the extra workload that is usually entailed in dealing with 'foreigners' who are buying properties in France.

2 How to find property in France

must know

Additional charges
Check that UK-based French
agents are not making any extra
charges – most reputable ones
will work on a share of their
associated agent's commission
so that the asking price is the
same as if you went direct to the
French agent – in effect, you get
the UK agency's assistance for
free. Don't be shy about asking
at the very beginning if they will
make extra charges for assisting
in any way. Their involvement
can also sometimes save you
money as they will negotiate
for you, and they will keep you
posted with suitable properties
until you are able to visit.

Specialist agencies

There are also UK-based agents who specialize in
a small area, which can be extremely helpful if you
know exactly where you want to buy although they
will not be so well qualified to make comparisons for
you between areas. Some of these agents are long
established whereas others have 'jumped on the
bandwagon' as property purchase in France has
become more popular. Make personal contact
with them to help you decide which route to take;
consider their helpfulness, knowledge, efficiency
and the properties they have to offer as well as any
additional charges if applicable.

How to get the best from agents

Here are some useful tips and guidelines that will
help you to get the best property information and
assistance from an agent prior to making a viewing
trip to France. Start off by giving the agent as much
information as possible although you may not want
to include all the elements of your ideal property;
they may make it impossible for an agent to find
one. Compromises will always have to be made. You
can discuss this with the agent when planning your
viewing visit and again when you meet them to talk
through your requirements before viewing.

What agents need to know

► Where you want to look – don't make the area of
your search too wide.
► Your maximum budget – if you want to see a wide
range of properties then tell them how low to go but
be honest about the maximum if you want to see
the best they can offer.

► Your minimum requirements – the size, number of bedrooms, condition and garden, etc.

► Style of property – old or new.

► 'Must haves' – anything that is so important to you that you would not buy a house without it, e.g. views, single storey, walking distance to shops, flat garden, not on a main road.

Useful guidelines

Having contacted a wide selection and presuming you are going to deal with a UK-based agent or agencies, it is best to choose one agency but if this proves difficult then a maximum of three should suffice.

► Do let the agents know your opinions on what they send you so that they can continue to help you and send properties that will appeal to you.

► Do give them ample time to arrange a viewing trip for you. Remember that appointments are going to have to be made with agents in France, most of whom spend a lot of time out of the office with clients, so confirmations of appointments may take a few days.

► Do tell them where you will be based, but if you are looking in a few different places, stay near to the next day's appointments and move on each night.

► Do tell them about other appointments you are making and which other agencies you are using so that there is no confusion or double bookings and they leave enough time for you to get to your appointment.

► Do allow enough time during your visit to explore the areas you are viewing in – it is almost more important to like the surroundings, the local village, shops, bars, restaurants and leisure facilities than it is to love the property – you can always change the house to suit you – but you cannot move it!

want to know more?

Take it to the next level...

► **Dealing with agents** 66
► **Viewing properties** 70
► **Purchasing procedure** 110

Other sources...
► **Look at the specialist French property and lifestyle magazines that are now on sale in many newsagents or available by subscription. See:**
www.francemag.com
www.livingfrance.com
www.efmag.co.uk
www.frenchmagazine.co.uk
www.french-property-news.com
► **Look in the press and on the internet for both UK- and French-based French property agents. See:**
www.latitudes.co.uk

3 Different properties

Let us take a look at the different properties available in France. Styles, layouts and building materials vary considerably between areas. Properties are built to suit the climate of the area, and most older houses were constructed with local materials, such as stone, brick or wood. Each area has its traditional styles, many of which have been moulded by necessity, such as smaller windows in the sunniest climates to keep the interior of a house cool. In the same way, the slope of the roof may vary to suit the weather – where snow is possible it must be able to support a heavy fall.

Why do you want to buy?

Decide on your main reason for buying a property in France and then you will be in a position to choose the type accordingly. The following three examples will give you food for thought.

must know

Use the locals
All local artisans – builders, plumbers, electricians – have to be registered with the town hall. It is worth using them as they will give you a 10-year guarantee on any works carried out. They are well-known local residents with a reputation to protect, and although it may be more difficult to deal with them in French, it is safer than using recently arrived ex-pats who have no registration, reputation or guarantee.

Types of property use

▶ Weekend use – you need an easy to 'lock up and leave' property, which is close to amenities as you will only be there for short trips. Ideally, it should come with the possibility of heating prior to your arrival – an old stone draughty cottage in northern France could take the whole weekend to warm up.

▶ Family holiday home – you will need plenty of accommodation and outside space will be important, especially in southern France. If this is your reason for buying, the space and facilities available may be more important than location.

▶ Permanent home – you need to be sure that all the everyday amenities and services you need are accessible to you.

Using the property

When you decide that you want to own a property in France you also have to consider what you want to get out of it. It will help the decision-making process tremendously if you know how you will want to use the property – as a holiday or permanent home, as an investment or to generate income. Let's start by discussing the different types of property available to help you decide what would suit your purpose best.

France is renowned for its selection of old properties which are full of character. Many have

been sympathetically renovated to retain their original features, but there are just as many that have been almost ruined by their modernization which has taken little or no account of their traditional style. Some properties are just a little shabby while others need total restoration, including re-wiring, re-plumbing and re-roofing as well as decoration.

This traditional stone property has been sympathetically restored inside and out to make it a desirable dwelling.

You need to decide how much you can afford and cope with as far as arranging for work to be done or doing it yourself. If you have had work carried out in your UK home, you will know that it always seems to end up going over budget and taking longer than expected. If you do not speak French, this will be an additional obstacle to successful renovation. You will need to get estimates for work and understand exactly what they include – just as you would in the UK.

Land and gardens

Think carefully about the size of the garden you would like. It sounds great to have a few acres, but remember that you will be responsible for the upkeep – do you really want to spend your whole weekend sitting on an electric mower or, worse still, pushing a mower or doing the weeding? Perhaps your dream of land might be satisfied with a smaller garden which is surrounded by fields or woodland that do not belong to you so that you get the benefit of the spacious view but without the responsibility and hard work of maintaining the land.

Outbuildings

In earlier years, these may have been barns and stables and sometimes they can be converted into living accommodation. If the buildings were previously used for this purpose, e.g. a group of houses that may have been utilized for staff accommodation, then you can go ahead and refurbish them and use them for your living accommodation. However, if they were agricultural buildings then you will need permission to change their use for this purpose. You will first need a *certificat d'urbanisme*, which permits you to use them as living accommodation, and then you will have to put in detailed plans to the local town hall to request detailed building permission.

Most vendors will agree to a clause in the first contract making it subject to getting the *certificat d'urbanisme*. The agent will normally do this on your behalf but it can take some months to obtain. If you just wish to use the buildings for general storage then no permissions are necessary.

Do bear in mind that converting an agricultural building into living accommodation can be very expensive, sometimes more so than building from scratch. Renovating a barn or some stables may end up costing more than you budgeted for – you will need to install all the services, floors, walls and ceilings, etc. – so make sure you can afford to do the work before you buy, especially if you will be relying

must know

Budget carefully
Be careful not to overspend so that you make your property too expensive to sell – each area will have a limit as to how much a property will fetch. If you install the very best of everything during your refurbishment the total cost of the purchase and works may come to more than you could recoup on selling the property. Be aware also that the cost of maintaining some lovely old houses can be higher than more modern ones.

on the income. Quite a few properties in France have an attic area which can easily provide further accommodation – this could be a cheaper way of creating more living space and you will only have to apply for permission if you are changing the outside of the property.

Chambres d'hôtes and gîtes

If you would like to earn some money from your property it is possible to let up to five rooms without having to apply for permission or to comply with complicated regulations. It is normal to supply breakfast and, if you are feeling ambitious, dinner can be provided, too! With the help of the *traiteurs* (shops that provide wonderful ready-prepared food that you only need to reheat, and sometimes will even deliver) it is possible to produce a meal to be proud of without too much effort. Providing your

must know

Certificat d'urbanisme
If you buy a property with some outbuildings that have not been used as habitable space and which are not attached to your house, you will need permission to change their use to living accommodation. You must obtain a *certificat d'urbanisme*, which allows you to change their use. Your agent will apply for you and your first contract (*compromis*) should contain a condition making it subject to you obtaining it.

A substantial property can provide you with a superb home and allow you to run a *chambres d'hôte* to increase your income.

must know

Buying an existing business
Purchasing an up-and-running
chambres d'hôte or *gîte* complex
will provide you with immediate
income as the property is not
only ready to use but, hopefully,
will already have a reputation
and a certain amount of good
will and repeat custom.

guests with food is more profitable and will add
a disproportionate amount to your earnings.

If you buy a property with more than one house
then you could let out the extra houses as *gîtes*.
These are self-contained units and all you have to do
is to provide clean accommodation for rental, i.e. on
changeover days you must clean them thoroughly,
providing a change of linen. Crockery, cutlery, etc.
must also be available for your guests. It is often
cheaper to buy a property with ready-made *gîtes*
giving you immediate income rather than have an
unknown cost for conversion. Bear in mind also that
it may take you six months to a year to complete the
work before you are in a position to earn any money
from the property – during which time your cash
flow will be strained.

Which services?

If you decide to go the *chambres d'hôte* route, you
must be prepared to have people – in fact, strangers
– living in your house with you. You need to be a
sociable type of person who enjoys company and
is happy to serve breakfast to them in your dining
room and allow them to sit in your lounge.

Letting out *gîtes*, however, will give you more
privacy but it will cost more to purchase a property
with separate living units and the income from letting
gîtes is lower per week as you are not providing the
same services, such as laundry and food.

In order to boost your income from *gîtes*, it is
a good idea to offer extra services to your guests,
including daily breakfast delivery, i.e. freshly-baked
croissants and bread, groceries on arrival, barbecue
evenings or meals served in the main house.

You may also consider providing other services, such as bicycle rental, art, wine or cookery courses, or whatever your speciality may be. Organizing golf, horseriding and walks are other options. Basically, the provision of a range of services is a good way to earn more money from your property.

A pool is almost essential if you are going to attract holidaymakers to rent a *gîte* – for B & B you might manage without one as you may attract more one-nighters but it would certainly help and may encourage longer stays which are more lucrative.

Renting out properties

If *chambres d'hôtes* and *gîtes* do not appeal as you value your privacy, you may like to earn some extra income through renting out a property or two. If so, you could consider buying one or more new small apartments or houses on a complex as they rent easily and offer low maintenance. You will know exactly what they are going to cost before you start, and you may be able to have a guaranteed rental.

must know

Location, location
Don't be tucked away too far off a tourist route – passer-by trade can boost your income. And remember that looks count; for rentals a pretty picture works wonders – flowers, pots and sunshine. A pool is also a great attraction but make sure that it complies with the new laws in France (see page 129).

This new development around a golf course is built in the style of the area. Houses such as this on golf courses are easy to let out throughout the year as golfers play in all weathers.

Old versus new

Many people start out with an idea of the house or apartment they would like but end up buying something totally different. You need to do your research to get the right property for you.

must know

Protecting the purchaser
French regulations regarding the purchase of new properties are very protective of the purchaser. The developer must have a bank guarantee in place to ensure that purchasers will get their property come what may; even if the developer encounters financial problems the bank guarantees that they will employ other builders and you will get your property. In practice, this means that developers do not run into problems as the bank will have done its due diligence before offering a guarantee.

What suits you?

You may fancy the idea of a 'chocolate box' country cottage surrounded by flowers and gardens, but in the event decide that cutting the lawn every weekend is not what you had in mind. Along with the charm and character of many old houses comes poor insulation and draughty rooms, so it may take the whole weekend to warm up your home, depending on which part of France you live in. Older properties may require continual maintenance which can be expensive, and this sometimes persuades buyers to opt for a newer house or even an apartment.

Some purchasers set out with the idea that a house needing renovation may be cheaper and then realize that they cannot cope with all the work and expense involved and buy a ready-to-move-into property instead. Other buyers who want a house in perfect condition may discover that they cannot find perfection and decide to restore one themselves.

Buying a new property

When you are buying a new property that has not been built yet (buying 'off-plan') you will need to be prepared to wait for it as, normally, building does not start until most of the development is sold. You can view the site and choose the orientation and size of home you prefer, but, obviously, the earlier you choose, the better the choice but the longer the wait until it is completed.

These developments tend to be built either near the coast or in particularly popular places a little inland; they are rare in the centre of rural France. Properties for investment may also be found in the major cities where demand for rental properties will be high.

Refurbished property

Occasionally developments of refurbished property come on to the market, in which case you will be able to view the building. Many of these developments were previously used and owned by large French companies for the purpose of staff holidays, but this practice seems to be dying out and such properties are often refurbished and offered for sale. These become available more quickly then new developments and offer the possibility of at least viewing the shell of the house or apartment.

Advantages of a new home

New developments especially appeal to the French and many other Europeans. They are built to comply with modern regulations and will have a 10-year guarantee which is similar to the National House Builders Guarantee in the UK. Because new homes have good insulation and use low-maintenance materials, the upkeep costs are likely to be low. In addition, they are ready to move into and offer the possibility of making new friends as most purchasers will take possession of their properties at around the same time, so it is an opportunity to meet like-minded people. They also provide friendly neighbours and friends for children to help get them speaking French.

In the UK in recent years, there has been a huge increase in interest in purchasing new properties in France due to the many benefits they offer. With UK property prices having risen so much, many would-be buyers have been priced out of the British market and, in order to get onto the property ladder, are finding that prices are more affordable in France, especially with these easy to lock up and leave properties. We have seen the prices of these properties continue to rise after purchase so that normally their value is even

must know

Reading plans
You need to have imagination and be able to read the plans. You will be able to view the site and situation of your property and will be shown exactly where it will be placed, but it is often hard to visualize the finished building within landscaped grounds when you're looking at a muddy field with no markings.

higher before they are completed and you take possession of them, making them an excellent capital investment.

However, you do need to be aware that many developers will increase prices every few months for the properties that have not yet been sold on a development. Once you have made your reservation, the price is normally fixed and will not be affected by any subsequent price increases. Prices for new developments are not negotiable.

Security and communal facilities

New properties or resale properties that are situated in a gated domaine or a block of apartments offer security which is wonderful if you are not going to be there all the time. Some have on-site caretakers who can be useful for not only keeping an eye on your property but are sometimes willing to turn on your heating and source a cleaner, gardener or any other service that you need. They often offer communal facilities, too, such as swimming pools, tennis courts, golf and gardens which are maintained for you. This service offers an ease of usage to those purchasers who do not wish to arrive at their home for a weekend of gardening and pool cleaning but still want access to all these facilities.

Building your own house

Many people are tempted to buy a plot of land, often in a rural location, on which to build their dream home. If you are considering this option, make sure that the plot in question has 'outline permission' to build.

If you dream of building your own home to a specific design, then it is possible to buy a plot of land in France that has 'outline permission' to build a house, and this might be one of the three following options:

1 A single piece of land with permission for one house of a certain size, i.e. the amount of square metres of habitable space will be defined. You will then need to find an architect to draw

must know

Basic guidelines
► Choose an architect carefully: a local one who is well known at the *Mairie* and knows everyone. It's not what you know but who you know that can apply here.
► Agree a fee before you start.
► Ask the architect to oversee the works and pay for this if you are not going to be on site throughout the building.
► Agree the cost and timing for payments and completion with the builders before you sign any contract with them.
► Budget for the extras. Builders will often quote for the building only so allow for decoration, bathroom and kitchen fittings as well as garden landscaping.

up plans to submit to the *Mairie* in order to obtain detailed planning permission. This will take around two months and, once received, you will have to display a sign on your land for another two months to give details of the size of the construction, etc. Meanwhile, you will need to obtain estimates from preferably three builders for the construction.

2 A *lotissement*, which is a group of plots of land that are situated together and being sold separately. The same facts apply as outlined above, but there will be several purchasers building at the same time and it might be possible to use the same builders, which may reduce the cost.

3 A plot of land where the vendor is selling several plots with the land and a house on it together at an all-inclusive price, i.e. you have the choice of which piece of land and there is a selection of designs, perhaps four or five, from which you can choose.

Buying a property in need of restoration

Many people choose to buy an old property that needs restoring for a variety of reasons, including the following most common ones: they may love working on a property and having a project on the go; they cannot find exactly what they want regarding internal requirements but love old houses; they cannot afford what they would like but are prepared to live in just one part of a property and gradually improve it; or they may believe they can make a profit by buying, restoring and selling it on. If you decide to proceed down this route, then it is essential to control your budget. You should be aware of house prices in the area in which you are buying and be careful not to spend more on the property than it will ever be worth after paying for the necessary restoration work.

Points to consider

If you are going to do the restoration work yourself, make sure that you are aware of any regulations for the utilities. Internal works in a property that is already a house (i.e. not an agricultural building or barn) normally present no problems regarding permission to change the internal layout, but if you want to move or add external features such as windows and doors you may need permission and will have to prepare plans to submit to the *Mairie*.

Extending the property

If you want to extend the property, you must check first that this will be possible. This depends on the percentage of property that is allowed to be built on your piece of land. It can range from 10 to 30 per cent, so for instance if you have 1,000 square metres and your allowance is 10 per cent then the total habitable area you can have will be 100 square metres. If the property is, say, 80 square metres then you can build another 20 square metres, but you will still have to apply for detailed planning permission.

If you have a reasonable-sized property, over 150 square metres of existing space, then you will need to commission an architect to submit the plans for you. Be prepared for a wait as the *Mairie* can take up to three months to give permission, and they will issue you with a reference number for your application. Once the permission is granted you will have to display a board outside your property for two months so that all the surrounding neighbours can see it. You can start work at this point.

Make sure you check that your plans to improve the property will not contravene any building regulations. Pay particular attention if it is a listed building in which case *Bâtiments de France* may have to be involved to approve any improvements or changes.

Get estimates where possible from local artisans. People who work and live in the area are more likely to be trustworthy and proficient; they have their local reputation to consider and will want to do a good job in order to continue to be recommended. Bear in mind that building works are notorious for turning out to be more expensive than expected or estimated, so do make some allowance for this in your budget. They can also take longer than anticipated, so allow for this, too.

Leaseback purchase

This is the purchase of a freehold property and the granting of a lease to a 'holiday company' which will pay you a guaranteed rental. This form of purchase can take several forms.

must know

Leaseback purchase
It is important that prospective purchasers understand the transaction and the advantages and disadvantages of this method of purchase so they can make an informed decision. Although this is an excellent deal for some people, it will not suit everyone.

What does it mean?

The lease will be for a period of nine to eleven years on a fixed rental, which is normally inflation linked. The rent is guaranteed and it will be paid by the holiday company regardless of whether or not they rent out the property at all times.

TVA (VAT) refund

If you opt for this method of purchase you will be able to claim back TVA, which is set at 19.6 per cent in France and normally included in the purchase price. This law was instigated to encourage more people to buy and rent out properties, but only newly built ones; TVA is not normally refundable on refurbishments. An example of how the system works in practice is if a property costs 100,000 euros inclusive of TVA, if you choose a leaseback purchase it will cost only 83,612 euros – a huge saving!

The TVA in some cases is paid and reclaimed by the developer – in which case it is never actually paid over by the purchaser. In other cases, the purchaser will have to pay the TVA and then reclaim it. This can take six to nine months so you will need to be able to fund the amount of the TVA for this period. In this case, the developer will usually provide assistance to reclaim the TVA – sometimes making a small charge to do so.

Personal use of properties

Some leaseback properties are designed solely for pure investment purposes and offer the purchaser no personal use – the guaranteed rental for these properties is normally a little higher and they are often found in the major cities where they are let to students or the general working population.

Other leaseback properties, however, offer you a small amount of personal use, which ranges from two to eight weeks normally. The percentage rental return is usually lower but you will need to add in to the amount of the rental the perceived cost of the weeks that you will be using the property. Therefore, as an example, if you think that the two weeks' use that you have would normally cost 1,000 euros then you should add this amount onto the guaranteed rent in order to calculate your true return on the property.

There are also leaseback purchase properties where all you need to do is give the holiday company a month's use of your property (you can use it up for up to six months). Although these properties offer a very small rental return it may cover some of the expenses on the property, and you will have a huge amount of personal use and will have also saved paying the 19.6 per cent TVA on the original price. The guaranteed rental will be set out in your lease (*bail*), normally as a percentage of the property's cost.

The amount of weeks available for personal use and the way they are arranged varies between developments, ranging from one or two weeks to several months and, in some cases, just a reduction on the rent being given whenever you want to use it.

must know

Check the following

▶ What the percentage rental is based on, i.e. the price including TVA or not (TTC or HT).

▶ If there are any service or maintenance charges to be paid or deducted from the rent.

▶ The cost of the furniture – for leaseback properties you have to purchase the furniture which is provided as it is essential that all properties on the development are decorated and furnished in the same way and to the same standard for rental purposes

▶ The *notaire*'s (conveyancing) fees.

▶ The agency commission: there should be no charge to you from the agency – they will be paid by the developer to assist you throughout the purchase.

When you are buying a leaseback, bear in mind that city centre locations give good rental return, often as accommodation for students, but are not always suited to holiday, permanent or personal use.

If you choose a development where you have some usage, you could calculate the cost of the property for holidays and add it into the equation of the rental return as you will not be paying for other holiday accommodation.

If you are working with limited holidays and time, then three to four weeks is probably as much as you would be able to use. You will not need to take responsibility for changing of linen and cleaning between renters; you just arrive at a perfectly cleaned holiday home on your allocated weeks and then leave it to the holiday company for the rest of the time.

Risk-free rental income

Bear in mind that in some seasons although the rental may be lower than you could get if you rented it yourself, you have no risk and you will receive your rent regardless of whether the

Frequently asked questions

Q: What if I decide to use the property full time or sell it and not renew the lease?
A: The TVA is refunded on the basis of a rental of 20 years. If at the end of your nine- or eleven-year lease you decide to sell or not renew, you will repay nine- or eleven-twentieths of the amount of TVA. Taking inflation into account, this will be a comparably small amount to pay back in nine years' time.

Q: What happens if I decide to sell the property within the period of the lease?
A: You can do so but you will have to sell it with the lease intact – to a like-minded buyer who is looking for an investment.

Q: What about the *notaire*'s fees?
A: On purchase, these fees will be as for any new property – around three per cent. If you buy a refurbished property being sold as a leaseback, then there is no TVA element in the sale and you will normally pay a deposit to reserve the property and the rest of the money will be due when the property is completed. *Notaire*'s fees will be seven to eight per cent of the price of the property, not the refurbishment cost, so they will equate to approximately five per cent of the purchase price.

Q: Is this method a good investment? I don't want to use the property myself.
A: Some leases give the purchaser no use of the property at all, and this suits some buyers who're looking for a pure investment, i.e. taking account of both the capital investment potential and the rental income. The potential capital increase is often forgotten by potential purchasers – they just look at the rental return – but the reason for buying leaseback is that your money is invested in property which historically increases in price – if you hold onto it for some time. Property is not for the short-term investor – although in recent years it has proved that it can be so.

Q: Can I take out a mortgage on a leaseback purchase?
A: You can take a mortgage, but not all banks will lend on them – it is wise to check with a mortgage broker specializing in French mortgages as to what you would be able to borrow on a leaseback purchase before you get involved with a purchase.

property is rented out or not. The company takes the risk and must allow for this. It is extremely unlikely that you could rent out all the weeks on your own.

You will have no concerns as to the security, maintenance and cleaning of the property. It is in the interests of the holiday company to keep everything in good order so that they can continue to rent as often as possible.

must know

Leaseback
Leasebacks that are purely for investment, i.e. student or worker accommodation, are not really suitable for personal use or permanent homes. They are exactly what they appear to be: an investment and only for letting.

Right of renewal

At the end of the nine- to eleven-year lease, rental agreements will give the right to renew to the holiday company. However, in practice they may not insist upon a renewal if it is not wanted, the reason being that if it became common practice to do so, it would make people wary about buying a leaseback property and they base their business on the continuing availability of properties. It may be possible to request a letter confirming they will not exercise their right.

Deposit and payments

You will pay a deposit of a maximum of five per cent of the purchase price and then pay the rest in stage payments (in exactly the same way as for any new property in France). To reserve the property you will sign a reservation contract and lease. The first stage payment is normally about 25 per cent and is payable once the foundations have been laid. The company can alter the lease prior to completion but should it change to any extent you have the right to withdraw.

Tax implications

You will require tax representation to declare the rental income in France; there is a tax treaty between the UK and France and you will not pay twice. You should declare the income in the UK if you remain a UK tax payer and will only have to pay more tax if the tax in the UK is above the amount you have paid in France, i.e. only the difference if there is any. In most cases the holiday companies can provide this assistance or recommend someone to you – there will be a small cost for this which should be borne in mind when you are calculating whether it is worthwhile for you.

Guaranteed rentals

As well as leaseback purchase for investment, some developments are offered for sale with a guaranteed rental possibility. These properties are sold in the classic way and may be purchased for permanent or holiday homes which the owners will use personally. They offer excellent potential if you wish to purchase for investment.

They are available with rental returns between four and five per cent guaranteed. They are let on a three year lease and must be let unfurnished. The rental company will make a charge for managing the property of around 6–9 per cent of the rental received, and will guarantee that should the property not be let, you will still receive the quoted rental. This costs three per cent of the annual rental. However, should the property be let for more than the guaranteed amount, you will receive the extra amount in full. The rental is also index linked.

This type of purchase gives you more freedom to sell or move in when you wish, but does not permit personal use. Because the development is lived in by many of the owners, it may be more saleable on the open market. Properties are usually well priced and compare favourably with leaseback properties with their TVA reduction.

want to know more?

Take it to the next level...

▶ **Renting out your property** 84
▶ **Leaseback purchase** 87
▶ **Buying a business** 178

Other sources...

▶ **If you are thinking of buying a property with** *gîtes* **and need to know what is required to get your property registered, see: www.gites-de-france.fr**
▶ **For more information on setting up a business in France, see: www.ccfgb.co.uk**
▶ **For an agent specializing in the sale of hotels,** *gîtes* **and campsites, see: www.leisureandland.com**

This artist's impression is of an ideal apartment block for permanent or holiday homes, or for permanent letting. It has balconies and set-in gardens but is also close to all the amenities and facilities of a large town.

4 Visiting properties in France

It is important to have some idea of what you would like to buy before you go to France to view some properties, but don't be too exacting as once you start hunting in earnest it is quite usual to change your ideas. Between two and six days is a practical length of time for a viewing visit – any longer and you will just become confused by what you are viewing and forget your original requirements. Looking at properties is also unbelievably tiring.

Be prepared

Arrange your appointments before you go, either through a UK-based agency or direct with a French agent. Remember that agents in France work on a fixed appointment basis and can get booked up some time in advance so don't leave everything to the last minute.

must know

Take advice
Do not base your visit on seeing particular properties – it is far better to let the agent know your requirements plus the properties you would like to see so that they can offer you all they have available. Once a sale is agreed, a contract is often signed immediately so there is no guarantee that a property you choose will remain available until you arrive. However, by the same token, new properties are coming on to the market daily and you may be offered something that was not available before you left the UK.

Properties can be spread over a huge area or can be difficult to view at different times of year, so make sure you allow enough time.

Decide on an area

Bearing in mind the size of France, don't try to cover too much ground when you decide on an area. It is absolutely useless to see lots of properties but have no idea of their surroundings – you need time to see the village or town and the surrounding areas to enable you to make a decision to purchase.

Always go to the area that is your first choice and 'do it to death' before looking elsewhere. If you really cannot find what you want there then you need to ask yourself the following questions:

▶ Is it because of your budget?
▶ Is it because you don't like the type of properties on offer there?
▶ Is it because the area doesn't offer you what you would like?

Only then, move on to your second choice. If you are not sure which areas to consider, it might be best to first visit all the ones on your list without viewing any properties in order to cover more ground and make a decision as to where to start viewing.

Organizing your trip

Make a decision as to whether you are planning your own trip and making appointments direct with French agents, or perhaps just taking a chance and

must know

Choosing an agent
Many prospective purchasers change their minds about what they require so it is more important that you make appointments with agents in the right area who can show you suitable properties rather than with agents who have one property that appeals to you – which by the time you get there may not suit your new ideas.

popping into agents. Alternatively, you may prefer to have everything organized for you in which case you will find it easier to use a UK-based agent or possibly two or three UK agencies. Don't use too many agents – UK agents are there to make your life easier. If you put your trust in one you will get the best service. If you are using more than one agency then do let them know so that there is no doubling up of appointment times or French agents as some of the UK agents work with the same French ones.

Most properties in France are offered for sale on a multiple agency basis, i.e. they are displayed with more than one agent in the area. You will also find that French agents will work with some of their competitors so that if they don't have a house to suit you they will contact other local agencies to see if they have something suitable and will then share the commission with the other agent and the UK agent – this will not cost you any more.

Private sales

You may wish to view a private sale that you have seen advertised, in which case, just let the agents organizing your trip know – they can then allow time for this whilst you are in the area. Bear in mind that with a private sale you will have to deal with all the negotiations, legal issues, estimates for work, utility changeovers, insurance, etc. yourself rather than have an agent organize these things for you, and although you save the agency fees you need to check that you are not paying over the odds for your property.

Making appointments

When you are making appointments for viewings, firstly, bear in mind that when you or your UK agency make an appointment with a French agent that it is a fixed one and that agent will be waiting for you, having not taken any other appointments for that time. If possible, a day or two prior to your departure, telephone and speak to the agent in France whom you will be meeting as this can often assist them in understanding your requirements

better. Although your agent in the UK will have passed on all the information they have, a personal call from you can also help.

This Provençal villa with its own private pool is ideal for long summer holidays with the family or for renting out when you are not using it.

Arrive on time

Do your best to arrive punctually and allow more time than you expect to get there – plan for tractors slowing down the traffic, getting lost, and finding the office and a parking space. It is far better to arrive early, in time for a coffee in the village or town to get the feel of things, than to arrive late, probably stressed and possibly at odds with your partner so that the visit gets off to a bad start. A phone call is always appreciated if you are running late or are lost.

In many cases agents will have arranged appointments with owners who may haven take time off work or driven some distance to be at their property, so if you arrive late you may have to deal with irate owners who have complained to the agent who, in turn, is under pressure to try to keep them happy.

must know

Sans nuisances
In French, this means without any problems surrounding the property, i.e. no smelly pig farms, noisy neighbours, railways, factories, main roads, etc.

Accommodation

It is a good idea to arrange not only your appointments but also hotel accommodation afterwards if you are going to cover a few areas. A good idea is to always stay near to the following day's viewing appointments. Most agents will be able to recommend somewhere suitable to stay. If you decide to rent a property for a week, it needs to be very central to where you are looking. Remember that you will be on the road looking at properties all day and will not want an hour's drive there and back at the end of each day. In holiday times, do make sure you make your arrangements for viewing and hotels a few weeks in advance to be certain of getting accommodation.

Discussing your requirements

When you arrive for your appointment in France, most agents will want to discuss your requirements in detail again before embarking on a series of house visits. Even though you may feel that you have given your UK agents all the information they would need to know it is often helpful for the local agent to hear it from you or to go through their properties so that you can point out the type of thing that appeals to you.

This can be a cause of consternation to some clients who feel all the ground work they did and choices that they have made as to properties they wish to view has been ignored, but an experienced agent will know that what you have chosen on paper and what you really want may not be the same thing. So often the properties selected do not comply in any way with the set of requirements given. As already mentioned, French agents' details do not have to be to the same standard as those of a British agent; they do not have to state that a property is by a railway or busy road, etc.

Do remember that you are a 'foreigner' in France, so don't try or expect to change the French estate agents' working habits. Try to put yourself in the place of the agent and vendor to understand that they will have to do a lot more for you than they would for their normal French clients.

Thus you may have expressed a preference for a quiet location but the property you chose to view is located on a busy road or in the centre of a village. Conversely, you may want to be right in the centre of a town offering a wide range of amenities but have chosen to look at a very isolated property. Some agents will just take you to see the property you have chosen regardless while others will discuss this with you in advance in order to save you both a wasted journey. You will discover that each agent will work in a slightly different way, as they do in the UK.

must know

Local customs
Don't always expect to be offered coffee when you arrive at the agency – it is not the norm in France – and don't be offended if they smoke without asking if you mind. Again, they are not being impolite; it is just accepted in France.

Bon de visite

Some agents will require you to sign this form prior to making visits to properties. This is just to confirm that they are taking you to see the properties listed; it does not commit you to anything. Normally they will keep one copy for their records, send a copy to the vendor and also give you a copy.

Follow French customs

Remember that you are a visitor in France and you need to go along with the way the French do things. Vendors sometimes change their minds about showing or selling, and properties get sold without agents being informed, so don't expect that just because you have come a long way or spent a lot of money getting there that they should do their job in a different way.

Lots of Brits who trod this path before you have not shown up, have been late for appointments, or have changed their requirements or budget having been to previous properties. You will get more help and commitment from the French agent by being polite and pleasant than by complaining – would you want to sell a house in your neighbourhood to an unpleasant foreigner?

Arranging appointments

When you are arranging your appointments, do bear in mind that the maximum number of agencies you can visit in one day is normally two: one in the morning and one in the afternoon. The French agent will often have additional properties to offer so a visit can take several hours. If you are making two appointments per day the agents will need to be close to each other and it is best not to mention to each agent that you are seeing the other. Be advised by your UK agency as to whether it is possible to fit in two appointments or not. They will have travelled the routes and will know the time it takes to drive between offices.

If your trip is long enough to allow just one appointment per day, this is ideal as it will give you time to see more of the area, have lunch there and take a wander around to make sure you like it.

Opening times

French agencies normally open at 9 or 9.30 am and close at midday for lunch. They re-open at 2 or 2.30 pm and many remain open until 6.30 or 7 pm. You will therefore need to make your appointments starting at the beginning of the morning or the afternoon. The agents are unlikely to accept appointments around midday.

In hotter weather, some agencies close for longer at lunchtime. Bear in mind that in the height of the summer it can be unpleasant to spend all day driving around in a car viewing properties – it is far better to view early in the morning and then wait until late afternoon before starting again. It is difficult to think clearly when you are really hot, and you will need to be in a position to make decisions reasonably speedily when you are out on the road viewing a selection of properties.

However, if you are out viewing with an agent, they will normally continue through the lunch break or suggest you stop and have a snack together. It is a good idea to make the suggestion of a break for lunch and even to offer to buy them lunch. Remember that bearing in mind that they are giving up their day for you as well as the cost of the petrol, it is little enough to offer them. It may also be a good opportunity to find out more about the area, the local property market and relative prices.

Viewing etiquette

Do not arrive at your appointment with the opening gambit of 'I only have an hour or two as I have another appointment somewhere else this afternoon'. This has the immediate effect of making the agent less interested in you and your search and they will feel that you are not putting your trust in them.

Many agents in rural areas have properties which may be 30 or 40 minutes' away from their offices so it can take about two hours to see just one property. Make sure you allow enough time to discuss your requirements with the agent so they know what sort of properties to take you to view – this will avoid wasting time going to look at unsuitable houses.

When you view a property, tell the agent your honest opinion of it; this will help them to find the right house for you.

Basically, remember that you are there to find a property and if the local agent accompanying you has various possibilities that could be suitable, then surely it is best to see all of them before proceeding elsewhere. You will also get a better overview of the area which is helpful in making a decision. If you decide that you don't like the area and would not be interested in a property there, then be honest with the agent without being rude about the region – perhaps something along the lines of 'thank you so much for showing us this property but unfortunately we can see that the area would not suit us after all'.

If you can see that the visit is going to take longer than you thought then phone to delay or cancel your appointment with the agent for that afternoon. Do this as early as possible so that they can rearrange their day – in this way you will not antagonise them and they will be happy to see you at a later date.

You will normally go out to view the properties in your agent's car. This is an ideal opportunity to learn more about the area – they will be happy to act as tourist guide. Put the time spent driving with the agent from one property to another to good use and ask as many questions as you wish about the area, the lifestyle, the amenities and leisure facilities, and the types of properties on the market, etc.

Whilst you are out viewing, it is important to give the agent your honest opinion of each property, as armed with this information they can often come up with suggestions that might suit you better. For instance, if you have planned to see three properties with them, all of a similar style and condition, and after seeing the first one you realize that it is totally wrong, you can save everyone a lot of time if you tell them this so that you can go straight back to square one and revamp your ideas and choices to enable you to see something that you think might be more suitable.

However always be polite to the owners if they are there and never say you don't like their house – wait till you come away! Don't think that you are unusual if you decide that what you thought you wanted could not be further from the truth – it happens more often than you would imagine and seeing the properties 'in the flesh' can be an eye opener.

Fixed appointments

If you are intending to fit viewings into your holiday, be aware that when you fix the appointments with agents they are fixed appointments and the agent will have cleared his diary for you, so that phoning five minutes before to say you cannot make it because the sun is shining, or you are too hot, or have been invited out for lunch, will not be taken kindly. The better way to arrange a trip which is part holiday and part viewing is to make sure you do all your viewing at the beginning of the trip, before relaxing into holiday mode. Keep to your appointments although, as stated earlier, leave some time free during the hottest part of the day to relax and think about what you have seen. Then when your viewings are complete, and having either found a property, or not, take your holiday.

must know

Bank holidays
Check the French bank holiday dates (see page 173) before arranging your viewing trip. Otherwise, you may find that the agents are closed.

Viewing in August

Bear in mind that the weather will be at its hottest and the traffic at its busiest in August, especially in southern France. Although most agencies will be available to show you properties you would be well advised to take this into consideration when making appointments. It is almost impossible to spend a whole day looking at properties in the heat – you will find that many agents in the South are happy to show you properties first thing in the morning and again perhaps after 4pm to avoid the hottest period of the day. Remember you are not just looking at properties – you are making one of the biggest decisions you will ever have to make, so do it with a clear head.

Also, viewing property in August may not give you the true idea of the area throughout the rest of the year. It won't be so hot all year round. Depending where you buy, the numbers of people around may drop considerably, especially English people, many of whom are just there on holiday. When all the crowds disappear you will be one of the 'locals' as far as the shops and neighbours are concerned and will feel far more at home.

Making up your mind

In today's market there is a risk that a property will be sold whilst you are still thinking about it. In years gone by you could feel fairly confident that if you planned to re-view a property in another month it would be there for you – now you cannot be so relaxed.

When you see a property that 'ticks most of your boxes', don't hesitate. These character property are very individual so it is unlikely that something similar will be waiting round the corner for you.

Committing yourself

Whilst visiting properties it is important to make notes; ask for a set of details on anything of interest. It is easy to come away and not remember which kitchen went with which living room and house, etc. Throw away any house particulars that are definitely not of interest so as not to cause confusion later on. If you really like a property, spend more time that day going back and cancel or postpone other appointments. Alternatively, arrange to go back the following day. Properties can sell quickly so make the agent aware of your interest. Making a verbal offer does not commit you, but don't do it if you don't mean it. Only when you have signed the contract and sent off the deposit and after your seven days' 'cooling-off' period are you then committed.

Follow up

Agents often get a new property in a day or so after a client has left, so always leave your contact number (mobile, local hotel or a friend in England whom you call each day where a message can be left for you) with the agents in the area you prefer. Or, at least, call them every day or two whilst you are in France in case they have seen anything else – this may be a waste of time but you never know.

On your return, if you have used British agents they will appreciate a call to let them know how the trip went – good or bad, successful or not. They will be interested to hear how you got on and your comments on the properties and agents. If you have not found anything suitable they can assist you again on another visit. Alternatively, if you have found a property, they can work with the French agent and assist you throughout the purchase procedure.

Property search dos and don'ts

Dos

1 Remember when in France, do as the French do.
2 Plan your trip with careful precision using an expert.
3 Arrive on time and expect to spend some time at the agent's.
4 Make time to see extra suggestions that the agents can offer as well as the area itself.
5 Be honest about your budget and requirements.
6 Tell the truth as to your impressions of each property but be mindful of the owner's feelings.
7 Do check what the price includes and if there are any additional costs to pay – taxes, *notaire's* fees and agency charges.

Don'ts

1 Don't try to cover too wide an area.
2 Don't try to see too many properties.
3 Don't rely on properties you chose to view prior to your trip still being available.
4 Don't be late for your appointments.
5 Don't tell agents that you are looking all over a huge area – imagine telling a UK agent you are looking at anywhere from London to Birmingham!
6 Don't forget to use your basic common sense.
7 Don't say everything is 'nice' when you don't mean it.
8 Don't forget to cancel unwanted appointments in good time.
9 Don't say you will come back or call if you won't.

want to know more?

Take it to the next level...

▶ *Régions* and *départements* 14
▶ **Estate agents** 39
▶ **Getting a mortgage** 78

Other sources...

▶ **Take advice from your agent regarding distances and how long it will take to reach an appointment, and use a route planner website:** www.viamichelin.com
▶ **For a list of agents across France who are members of FNAIM (association of French estate agents) see:** www.fnaim.fr
▶ **For estate agents in the UK that deal with foreign properties, see:** www.naea.co.uk
▶ **For a list of specialists in the international property market, see:** www. fopdac.com
▶ **To find a selection of bed-and-breakfast places to stay in France while you are property hunting, see:** www.chambresdhotes.fr
▶ **For a selection of reasonably priced hotels throughout France, see:** www.accor.com

5 Getting your finances in order

Before you embark on your search, you need
to know how much you can afford to pay.
If you have the cash available, it's simple, but
if you have to sell a property in order to raise
the cash, then it is probably best to get it under
offer before making visits to view. When you are
collecting information, be realistic about how
much you are likely to receive for your property
allowing for costs. You may decide to raise
money against your property in the UK,
so get this arranged prior to your search.

Arranging a mortgage

If you intend buying a property in France with a mortgage, then make enquiries and get an 'in principle' offer prior to starting your search, so that you are not disappointed at a later stage.

must know

Mortgage applications
You will need to provide the following information with your mortgage application:
▶ Copy of your *compromis* (contract of reservation).
▶ Your P60 or three months' salary slips.
▶ Copies of bank statements for the past three months.

Sterling or euro mortgage?

If a mortgage is required it is generally more prudent to fund your purchase by means of a euro mortgage. This reduces the risk of fluctuations in exchange rates. As an example, if the net equity is 150,000 euros (£100,000) – property cost, less mortgage – in a property costing 450,000 euros (£300,000) when exchange rates are 1.5 euros to the pound, it requires a mortgage of 300,000 euros (£200,000). A change in exchange rates has a different impact on net equity depending on the currency of the mortgage. Let us assume that exchange rates move to £1.667. The property is then worth £270,000 and with a sterling mortgage of £200,000 the net equity has reduced by £30,000 to £70,000. The same property with a euro mortgage has an unchanged net equity in euros of 150,000 which, converted to sterling at the new rate, translates to £90,000, a reduction of only £10,000. Had exchange rates moved in the opposite direction then the reverse would be true.

Getting a euro mortgage

To obtain a euro mortgage, you can apply direct to a French bank – some have offices specifically set up for UK buyers – but you need to understand the criteria for obtaining a mortgage in France. If your financial or personal set-up is quite complicated or you would like the process handled for you, it may be worthwhile to approach a mortgage broker specializing in French mortgages. They will know which banks will lend on certain types of properties and areas. They can submit an application to the most suitable bank and provide them with the requisite information. This can save you a lot of time and aggravation.

French banks specify that you can pay up to one-third of your monthly income in mortgage repayments. For example, if your income per month is £1,000 and your mortgage repayments in the UK are £200 then you will be able to borrow an amount which you can pay back at the maximum rate of £133 per month. The amount you can borrow with this repayment will depend on the length of the term for the loan and the rate you are offered.

Types of mortgages

There are different types of mortgages, some with fixed rates and fixed terms and others that are more flexible but possibly at a higher rate. You can usually borrow up to 80 per cent of the cost of the property, sometimes even more, although the rate may increase.

must know

Opening a bank account
If you are taking out a mortgage on your French property you will need a French bank account. Even without a mortgage you will need an account to pay your utility bills, etc. The bills can be sent to your permanent address in the UK and the money taken by direct debit from your French bank account a week or so later. Open an account when you have chosen a property and know where it is situated so your bank is accessible when you are in France. You will require proof that you own a property in France in order to open the account. The *notaire* can give you an *attestation* to show this.

New properties
If you are buying a new property and have to make stage payments, the bank will expect you to pay the amount that you are contributing to the purchase first and they will then take over the subsequent payments. However, they will check with you each time a payment is required to ensure that you are happy for it to be paid so that you can check on the progress of the property first if you want to.

Properties needing restoration
If you are buying a property to restore and would like a loan to pay for the works then you will have to get estimates from qualified local builders and tradespeople and submit these to the bank. You may have to prove that you have the personal funds to make the purchase – they will not want to lend for renovation if you don't have the money to buy the property.

Notaire's fees and taxes

These are paid by the purchaser. They are the French equivalent of solicitor's costs and stamp duty in the UK except the *notaire* reports to the government, charges a fixed fee based on the regulations and is the property tax collector for the government.

must know

Insurance
Insurance of the property is not your responsibility until completion and you may be able to take over the vendor's policy or ask your agent to organize this on completion as well as contents insurance. Alternatively, there is the possibility of a comprehensive Lloyds of London policy which is written in English.

Other costs

There are no other purchase costs. The agent's commission is included in the price of the property and is sometimes charged to the purchaser. This is actually a benefit as your *notaire's* fees and taxes will be based on the price you pay for the property. If you are paying, say, 105,000 euros for the property but the contract

It might be worth taking out a slightly larger mortgage to purchase a restored property. It can save money in the long run as you never know how much improvement work will cost.

states that the price is, say, 100,000 euros and the fees are 5,000 euros, then you will pay the *notaire's* fees and taxes on 100,000 only instead of on 105,000 euros.

Annual taxes

You will be responsible for paying the equivalent of annual council tax on the property. There are two of these: those collected by the local council and those collected by the government – *taxe d'habitation* and *taxe foncière*. They are collected annually in arrears and they are usually lower than for comparable properties in the UK. For new properties, you have the first year free.

Notaire's fees and taxes

▶ When buying a new property off-plan the amount charged will be 2.5–3.5 per cent, and should you decide to sell within the first five years your purchasers will pay approximately 2.5–3.5 per cent, too.

▶ When buying a property that is under five years old from the first purchaser who originally bought off-plan, the amount charged will be approximately 2.5–3.5 per cent.

▶ When buying a property over five years old, the amount charged is between 6.5 and 10 per cent. This amount is based on various factors and is calculated by the notaire. However, generally the cheaper the property the higher the percentage, i.e. a property priced at 50,000 euros is likely to have costs of nearer 10 per cent whereas a property at 500,000 euros is more likely to be nearer 6.5 per cent. The reason for this difference in taxes between old and new properties is that new ones have TVA (VAT) included in their prices, so no tax (stamp duty) is payable.

▶ When buying with a mortgage (*hypothèque*) the *notaire* will make a further charge to register the lenders' interest and act for the lenders on the property, i.e. take a charge on the property for the lender – this will be approximately 1.5 per cent of the mortgage amount.

▶ You may have furniture to buy and/or removal costs. You may also have to do a little work on the property. However, remember also that, say, 5–10,000 euros extra on your mortgage over 10 years may not cost very much to borrow and may allow you to find what you are looking for.

Buying euros

When you agree to buy a French property, the price will be in euros. The actual cost (in sterling) of the property depends upon the exchange rate that you achieve to buy the euros.

must know

Pensions
If you retire to France you can arrange to transfer your pension. This means you can relax as you won't have to talk to your UK bank from France and, like the mortgage payments, you only have to re-establish the facility every two years. It means that you can fix the amount of euros arriving in your French account each month which will make budgeting easier.

Exchange rates

It may seem obvious but often people are shocked by the cost implications of a sharp move in the rate. Once your offer on the property is accepted you are exposed to a currency risk until you secure an exchange rate. If you wait until funds are required in France, the cost of the property will fluctuate on a daily basis (becoming cheaper or more expensive).

To illustrate this we can look at a recent example: a watermill in Brittany priced at 400,000 euros would have cost £263,160 in August 2004 but increased to £275,862 by mid October (4.8 per cent in just 10 weeks). This is unnecessary and easily avoided. It goes without saying that the reverse could happen and your property could become cheaper if the euro were to weaken but if you are happy with the cost at the time of your offer you would be well advised not to speculate and risk paying more, i.e. to fix your rate.

How to buy euros

You have several ways of buying your euros. You will have to buy the deposit straight away and then must decide on a strategy for the balance.

▶ If you have all of the funds available for the balance you can buy euros straight away and hold them. You can then send funds to France as and when required.

▶ If your funds are tied up or you have not received any money yet from a UK re-mortgage you can fix an exchange rate for all of your future payments using a forward currency contract. This means that you can buy euros now but pay for them later (you will need to pay for only 10 per cent of the reserved currency straight away and the 90 per cent balance each time you need to make a euro transfer).

▶ You can wait and ask your currency broker to watch the rate for you. It is usually best to decide on the 'worst rate' you are prepared to accept and stick to this so that if things go wrong you do not go below a certain level. You can also establish a target price, which should be realistic and not too 'greedy'.

▶ If you are buying in a new development you will have stage payments to make and this makes it even more vital to fix an exchange rate at the outset as your time frame is much longer.

Shop around

It is a good idea to shop around when you are buying currency. Do not just assume that your bank will give you a good exchange rate, but equally don't assume that the cheapest broker will be the best either. You need to find a broker who will offer competitive prices and a high level of personal service and who will have an efficient payments team so that your money arrives safely and on time.

Regular payments to France

It is also worth talking to your broker or bankers about sending monthly payments to France. It is possible to find a currency service for transferring funds on a regular basis where the transfer fee is free. This may be a useful arrangement if you are thinking of moving to France permanently.

Mortgages

You can fix an exchange rate for up to two years ahead, then establish a direct debit with your UK bank and send your mortgage payments to France automatically. However, you must not miss a mortgage payment in France so do not leave it to chance.

Renting out your property

You may wish to buy a property as a buy-to-let investment so you need to be aware of the regulations regarding leases. Deal with an agent for this; they will find a suitable tenant and take references, which gives you a certain amount of protection.

must know

Rentals to students
Tenancy by a student may be considered seasonal if it is solely for the academic school year, and it is essential that the contract includes a provision to this effect. If such a clause is present, the student must vacate the premises in full on the date agreed in the contract.

Rental properties will need to be close to amenities if you want to rent them out throughout the year. For holiday lets, swimming pools and leisure facilities are more important.

Renting furnished accommodation

Furnished tenancy is governed by different legal and tax regulations from those that apply to unfurnished accommodation. You need to know more before making the investment. Consult an agent who deals with rentals in the area in which you are buying and who will find a tenant for you, prepare the contracts for rental, collect the rents, and even possibly manage the property for you – in exactly the same way as you would deal with a buy-to-let in the UK. Check with a rental agency before agreeing to buy an investment property that it will be easy to rent out at a suitable price. They will be able to take up references of the tenant for you and deal with the various legalities which you can also check with the *notaire*.

Many agents deal with both sales and rentals and can offer you suitable properties that they know they will be able to rent out easily and profitably. If you are working through a UK agency they will arrange for you to meet with their agents who offer this service.

Remember that tenants are not always careful and therefore you must conduct a schedule of condition and an inventory of the furniture with each change of tenant. As with any undertaking, there are pros and cons to be considered. Check the laws in place regarding rentals.

Leases

These must be for a period of at least three years, and owners must give tenants six months' prior notice before removing them from the residence. Tenants may be removed only for their failure to comply with their responsibilities or in the event that the lessor must regain possession of the residence in order to live in it or sell it. Such a contract will include the length of the rental, the procedures for giving notice, the amount of rent and the procedure for setting it, and liability for repairs.

Inventory and schedule of condition

Each party to the agreement is responsible for assessing any change in the condition of the furnishings on the basis of a precise and detailed inventory of the furniture. This document is attached to the lease contract. Unless a schedule of condition is performed, the property is deemed to have been in good condition. The tenant may therefore demand a schedule of condition if the lessor does not offer to conduct one.

Holiday rentals

If you wish to rent out your property when you are not using it, normally for the purpose of holidays, you can do so. There are several ways of doing this: you can approach a local French agency, which works well if your property is in a popular holiday area; you can go to one of the holiday companies in the UK that prepare brochures on holiday rental accommodation; or you can advertise in one of several brochures where you just pay to advertise your property so that interested clients will contact you direct to make the arrangements. You can also advertise privately in the national, local press or some of the UK French property magazines if you are willing to deal with the potential clients yourself. It will depend on how often you want to let it out, whether you are living close by or in the UK and the type and size of property you own as to which route you take.

Benefits of renting out

Renting out your property may mean that you are able to purchase a better or larger property in the first place, using a mortgage that can then, in effect, be paid off by your tenants. Many people go this route in order to achieve what they want and once the mortgage is paid off they can stop renting out their home.

You may decide to rent it out for a short time each year to cover the expenses and perhaps the notional interest on the money invested in the property so that apart from the initial purchase cost you have free accommodation. Or, you may wish to carry out works to the property and can accumulate the money to do so by renting it out.

Leaseback purchase and rental

This gives the purchaser either full rental return or rental and personal use. The return on these arrangements can be lower as it is the leaseback company and not the vendor that is taking the risk on whether they will find a tenant for the property.

Self Invested Pension Plans

In April 2006 in the UK, there will be new rules governing SIPPs (Self Invested Pension Plans) which will allow the purchase of residential property, including overseas property, by the plan as long as it is for investment purposes, i.e. it generates an income which is paid into the pension fund.

This is new legislation so it is extremely important that you take advice from your financial advisor as to what your pension administrator will allow once the legislation has been ratified. In principle, the money you pay into your SIPPs is tax deductible and it is this money that can be used to invest in property. The income received is not taxed within the fund, thereby building up the fund more quickly. It is anticipated that you will be able to borrow up to 50 per cent of the purchase price on the basis that your fund has the other 50 per cent.

want to know more?

Take it to the next level...

▶ *Gîtes* and *chambres d'hôtes* 47
▶ **Leaseback** 56
▶ **Signing the final contract** 136
▶ **Property taxes** 90

Other sources...
▶ **For currency brokers, i.e. buying euros, transferring money for purchase, or regular payments, see: www.hifx.co.uk**
▶ **To access a list of *notaires* and get more information about their functions and what they do, see: www.notaires.fr**
▶ **For a mortgage broker who specializes in mortgages for properties in France: www.charleshamer.co.uk**

6 Taxes and maintenance charges

This chapter focuses on the property and other taxes that you may have to pay as well as giving you valuable information about maintenance costs and service charges if you are planning to buy in a complex or block of apartments. If you are thinking of moving to France permanently and becoming a French tax payer then you must take advice from a qualified accountant as tax laws are continually changing.

Property taxes

There are two taxes on all residential property. These are collected by the state for the local authorities and assessed at individual rates according to the location; thus they can vary substantially. Ask your estate agent for details when you are viewing properties.

must know

Taxation treaty
As a UK tax payer you must declare any capital gain on a property on your UK tax return. There is a double taxation treaty between France and the UK so you don't have to pay taxes twice but will have to pay the higher of the taxes calculated under each treaty. Thus, if under French tax law you are required to pay 10,000 euros (approx. £6,600) and when you make your declaration in the UK the tax is calculated at, say, £9,000, you will only have to pay the additional £2,400 in the UK.

Taxe foncière

As the owner of a property on the first day of January, you are liable for paying this tax (rates paid to the government) which is due for payment by October/November. Penalties or fines are added for late payment. It is possible to arrange a monthly payment scheme at the outset. Sometimes the vendor may ask that you pay a proportion for the number of months left.

Taxe d'habitation

This local tax (the rates paid to the *commune* or town) is only due on a habitable building. The occupant of the property on the first day of January is liable for paying this tax, even if you only use the property occasionally, if it is furnished and supplied with water and electricity. The amount of this tax will vary from one place to another and according to the size of the property.

If you rent out your property to someone else and they are living there on the first day of January for the year, they are liable for paying the tax. However, the person in occupation must have a lease and be semi-permanent; if you are just doing short-term holiday lettings, you will be responsible for paying this tax.

Capital gains tax

With regard to tax matters you should always take professional advice as each person's financial situation can vary and laws can change. Capital gains tax for a main residence is not payable in either country – France or the UK. It is only payable on any gain you make after various allowances as mentioned below. It is not anything to worry about; after all, if you come out with a gain and have to pay a little tax on it, you are still left with a substantial profit. If the property was a second home, it will have provided you with holidays and enjoyment. Remember that the more tax you have to pay, the more profit you will have made.

In France, since 1 January 2004 capital gains have become fully tax-exempt after 15 years of possession, instead of 22 years under the previous law. Specifically, a 10 per cent reduction would be applied per year of possession of the property after the fifth year. It is a simple calculation: if the real estate sold and the property was purchased by the seller 15 years earlier, you then multiply 10 per cent

Buying a property in a more built-up area can give you a better capital increase as the population is higher, thereby creating a greater demand for property.

by 10 years to yield a 100 per cent reduction in the tax assessed on the seller's capital gains. If the seller purchased the property 14 years earlier, the reduction is 10 per cent x 9 years = 90 per cent. In this case, only 10 per cent of the capital gains will be taxed.

In addition, the new law simplifies the method used to calculate capital gains by eliminating the monetary depreciation factor and by applying a flat surcharge of 15 per cent of the purchase price for construction work if the sold property was in the seller's possession for more than five years. Taxpayers can substitute their actual expenses for this flat 15 per cent deduction if they provide proof of their expenditures – this must be in the form of invoices from bona fide tradesmen only.

Don't forget that length of ownership is calculated in 12-month periods. You should also bear in mind that a fixed deduction of 1,000 euros is applied to capital gains earned on a transaction.

Exemptions

A primary residence is exempt with no requirement on the length of occupancy. In order to qualify for this exemption, the building must serve as the seller's main residence on the day of the transfer. For non-residents, i.e. French citizens and EU nationals residing outside the country, they will receive an exemption on their residence in France if they have paid taxes in France for two consecutive years at some point in the past. Don't forget that any assets for which the selling price is less than or equal to 15,000 euros do not qualify for the exemption.

Calculating and paying the tax

Among the more significant changes since 1 January 2004 is the new method used for calculating the capital gains tax as well as the new payment procedures. The tax is due immediately, at the time of sale. The law requires *notaires* to prepare the return on the seller's behalf and to file the payment. The tax rate and calculation methods defined for residents of France will apply to EU nationals subject to

This lovely old stone property situated on the outskirts of a town is typical of the traditional homes that you can buy.

income tax as well. For other non-residents (i.e. non-EU nationals), the tax rate would remain at the current 33 and a third per cent. Calculation of capital gains tax in France and the UK does differ so make yourself aware of the laws in both countries before you put your French property on the market. Tax laws can change continually so ensure that you get up-to-date information. The tax rules may vary considerably for non-EU nationals.

Important

Finally, keep in mind that all the information to be submitted in the capital gains tax return must be provided to your *notaire* along with the original copies of any supporting documentation. If anything is missing, the tax authorities may automatically apply interest for late payment to your tax liability.

Keep a copy of every transaction regarding your property and any works you may have carried out in your records and ask your *notaire* to go through the whole process with you before a projected sale, so as to avoid any unpleasant surprises. If you need further information about tax and the regulations that may apply to you personally, consult an accountant who specializes in French tax affairs.

Maintenance and service charges

Properties in France are purchased freehold in all cases. If you are buying a property in a complex or a block of apartments then you will become a co-owner – or *copropriétaire*.

A communal pool will increase the value of your property, attract higher rentals and is almost essential in southern France.

The management company

You, along with all the other owners, will be in control of the management company running the development and they cannot make charges to you without prior agreement from the *copropriétaires* who will have formed a tenants association.

If you are purchasing a property such as an apartment within a complex, there are maintenance and service charges to pay. You should consider these charges before signing the *compromis*. The charges will vary according to the size and quality of the complex, whether there are lifts, a swimming pool, gardens, tennis courts and other facilities. They will normally be calculated on a per square metre basis so the larger your property the higher the charge.

Syndics and *copropriétaires*

The owners and the elected management of a building which is owned jointly by individual owners of apartments within that building have certain responsibilities. French law defines in great detail both the rights of the apartment owners within a *copropriété*, i.e. a residence or complex or building split into separate and physically distinct apartments, as well as their responsibilities to other owners. These are detailed in the volume of rules and regulations that each owner should receive from the *notaire* at the same time as the title to their property.

The *syndic*

The *syndic*, or managing agent, is both the manager of the building and the regulator of relationships between owners, service suppliers and the insurance company responsible for the *dommage ouvrage* (the 10-year 'building defects liability insurance' that must be taken out by the developer of any apartment building). The *syndic* is appointed by the co-owners.

Duties of *copropriétaires*

It is the responsibility of each owner to understand the rights and the responsibilities detailed by the statutes, and to ensure that they, their families, servants, suppliers and tenants respect them.

▶ The day-to-day safety and management of an apartment building, as well as its long-term preservation, are the joint responsibility of all the owners of the apartments within a building defined as a *copropriété*.

▶ If you buy an apartment with the intention of renting it out, you need to notify the *syndic* of your permanent address since you, as owner, remain

If you are considering buying into a complex with a communal pool, as shown in this artist's impression, the management company will take responsibility for the pool. It will give you the opportunity of getting to know your neighbours better.

responsible for your tenant's behaviour and the payment of all service charges. The *syndic* does not recognize tenants, only owners with title.

▶ The owner is responsible for paying the service charges due on the apartment and its dependencies, such as the storerooms and parking area, and the law on payment is now very strict.

▶ Each year the owners agree a budget with the *syndic* for the management cost of the whole building. Each apartment, store room and parking place represents so many shares of the whole and this is the basis of the service charge assessment of the individual owner. Based on this estimate, a provisional demand is sent to owners on the first day of the current quarter and this is immediately payable. In the event

that this demand is not met, then all service charges due
for the current fiscal year become due and payable. The
defaulting owner must then pay all the collection charges,
including legal fees. The final sanction is sale of the apartment
to meet these expenses.

Assemblée Générale (AG)

The owners must hold at least one AG (General Assembly) per
year, at which they will:
▶ Decide what needs to be done for the maintenance, repair
or improvement of the building.
▶ Agree a budget to cover the cost of this work for the current year.
▶ Approve the spending of the budget of the previous year, and
then accept the completed accounts.
▶ Dismiss, approve or re-appoint a *syndic* to act as the executive
authority of the owners.
▶ Elect from their number a smaller group to act as adviser
to the *syndic* – the *Conseil Syndical* (CS).

Authority of the *syndic* (managing agent)

Under French property law, only the *syndic* has the executive
authority and the legal power to:
▶ Collect the service charges agreed at the AG, generally on
a quarterly basis, and to proceed legally against those owners
who have not paid.
▶ Levy additional funds over and above the normal budget as
agreed at the AG.
▶ Enter into contractual commitments with the major utilities,
such as water and electricity, as well as cleaning firms, builders
of various types and service suppliers, such as TV installers,
gardeners or swimming pool maintenance firms.
▶ Spend money on the building and its needs, unforeseen in
the annual budget but subject to an upper limit and sometimes
the agreement of the *Conseil Syndical* (CS).

Exterior of buildings

Generally, but not always, the rules of behaviour stipulate that the exterior appearance of a building, including any windows and doors that are part of the external appearance of individual apartments, cannot be altered either by paint or physical modification without the written agreement of the *syndic*. This is also true of other exterior modifications to private apartments, such as roof gardens, or a satellite TV dish.

Interior of buildings

Owners may carry out any modifications that they wish to the interior of their apartments at their own expense but subject to the design and monitoring of a licensed architect and the approval of the planning authorities and the written approval of the *syndic* that all these necessary procedures have been met.

Responsibilities of the *syndic*

A *syndic* can only act within specific proposals previously agreed by the AG, and within the limits of the budget voted for that purpose.

▶ The *syndic* must keep all necessary records of the building, including the addresses and voting rights of owners, changes of ownership of apartments within the building, insurance and service contracts, and payments authorized and made.

▶ The *syndic* should ideally maintain a separate bank account for the building and this separate bank account must itemize all sums paid in and out on behalf of the building.

▶ The *syndic's* accounts of the building itself must show an up-to-date record of all service charges and especially any arrears.

▶ The *syndic* also needs to keep insurance records. These are both for claims and payments under the building defects liability insurance – such as a leaking roof, cracking terrace or rotten drains – and for claims between owners.

▶ The *syndic* is required by law to obtain three competitive quotes for any significant service/work/contract.

▶ If as an owner you are dissatisfied with the maintenance contractor – or anyone else for that matter – who is hired by the *syndic*, complain first to the CS and, if that is unsatisfactory, to the *syndic*. If that fails, and others share your concerns, request that this is put on the agenda of the next AG.

▶ The *syndic* is responsible for calling the AG within six months of the financial year end of the *copropriété*, and delivering to all owners 15 days before the AG the completed accounts for the previous year, a budget for the coming year, and an agenda for discussion at the next AG.

▶ Within six days of the receipt of the Agenda, owners can require the *syndic* by registered letter to add items to the Agenda of the AG. Remember that matters not on the Agenda cannot be discussed at the AG, and any discussions or decisions on such matters have no legal authority.

▶ The *syndic* must make available on a defined day after the calling of the meeting but before the AG itself, all records of the *copropriété* for any owner who wishes to inspect them. In addition to the bank records, these records must include the supporting documentation for the common expenses, such as invoices, contracts, and the general ledger.

▶ The *syndic* acts as secretary to the AG, and sends out to all owners the *procès-verbal* (minutes of the meeting) within a maximum three months of the holding of the AG. These minutes must show those owners physically present and those represented, decisions taken and votes in favour and against each decision.

▶ The *syndic* also has the authority to take such actions as are necessary to preserve the integrity of the building, especially where the action or inaction of an owner is causing, or may cause, problems. Where possible the *syndic* will notify such owners by registered letter before any such action is taken. If the urgency of the situation does not allow that time, the *syndic* has the right to enter such an apartment and carry out whatever work is needed at the expense of the owner.

Harmony of the building

The harmony and effectiveness of any *copropriété* depends crucially on successful communication between the *syndic* and the owners, as well as successful management of the common parts of the building. Replacing broken lights, ensuring clean and tidy garbage collection, good maintenance of communal, gardens, effective functioning of lifts and garage doors and, above all, regular cleaning are minor issues in themselves but major sources of dissatisfaction.

This communication task is normally the function of a *Conseil Syndical* (CS) or Management Committee of Owners. Owners elect the CS from amongst their members. At the AG two of these normally act as President of the Meeting and Scrutineer of the Votes, with the *syndic* acting as Secretary of the meeting. The CS has no executive authority but acts as

Management companies normally insist that balconies are uniform and blinds, if allowed, are of the same material.

adviser to the *syndic*, and as the main communication link between the owners and *syndic*. In certain circumstances, individual members of the CS also act as agents for the *syndic*, taking specific responsibility for overseeing the cleaners of the building and the gardeners, etc. Members of the CS are elected at the AG.

Choice of *syndic* – amateur or professional?

Any building with multiple apartments needs a *syndic*, but they do not have to be professionals – they can even be one of the owners of the apartments. The main law governing *copropriétés* is that of 10 July 1965 as amended by that of 13 December 2000. Any *syndic*, whether a professional or an amateur, will require a full understanding of these laws since the *syndic* carries considerable responsibility in terms of the law and third party insurance liability. A professional *syndic's* mandate is for three years and it is renewable.

The job of a *syndic* is, generally, a thankless task – they get more brickbats than bouquets! Naturally, it is also one that requires a great deal of attention to detail and bureaucratic paperwork. Owners do not like to pay for this, so *syndics* often under-estimate their fees, and then they make up for this by over-charging on services and necessary maintenance and repair work to the building.

Bad or inefficient *syndics* are more often than not the fault of an inadequate CS. Buildings need regular maintenance and good buildings have owners who are willing to devote time and money to the protection of their investment.

Pricing depends upon the complexity of the building, its immediate problems and the anxiety of a *syndic* for extra work. It is unlikely with the amount of paperwork involved that any *syndic* can cover their costs at a fee of less than an annual 100 to 150 euros per apartment, and the owners have to be prepared to pay for this.

This older apartment block has character. The fact that the owners have control of how the property is maintained means that everything is in good repair.

Bringing about change

Owners who are dissatisfied with their building should always remember that they are in France – the country of 'direct action' and *liberté*, *égalité* and *fraternité*.

▶ You can canvass your neighbours' views on the running of the building. Identify the key complaints, which owners will support you and, even more important, those who will work with you.

▶ You can approach the CS informally with these complaints, and your suggestions for change and improvement. Suggest that some, or all of you, be co-opted onto the CS with the intention of being elected at the next AG, replacing or adding to the existing CS.

▶ If the existing CS will not resign, nor cooperate, write officially to the *syndic* requesting that the enclosed list of owners be proposed for election as the CS at the next AG. Should this request not be on the proposed agenda when it is distributed, send a further registered letter within the six days that are allowed after the receipt of the agenda.

▶ You should ensure that your supporters either turn up at the AG or send in their proxies. Remember that no one single owner can represent more than three others at an AG, but also that a proxy for an owner does not have to be an owner himself/herself. Ensure that the *syndic* registers both your own attendance and your proxies at the start of the AG.

▶ Voting for members of a CS is a simple majority of the owners present and represented.

▶ With the new CS in place, meet the *syndic* to discuss your complaints about the running of the building, and your suggestions for change. The *syndic* cannot agree to any major expenditure not approved by the AG, but can exceed the approved budget by not more than 10 per cent for items of immediate importance.

▶ Neither owners nor the *syndic* are keen on more than one AG a year, so improvements involving money will have to wait for a year. In this time, the CS and *syndic* can get to know each other, identify the problems and decide whether they can work together.

▶ If the CS decides that it cannot work with the existing *syndic*, then the ultimate sanction is replacement. A new *syndic* can only be appointed at an AG.

A good investment

The value of your investment is your responsibility, and good maintenance at a reasonable price is obviously of importance. You do not have to get involved – you can leave it all to your neighbours – but it will give you an opportunity of really getting to know your co-owners in the building, and your French will also improve in the process of speaking to everyone.

want to know more?

Take it to the next level...

▶ **UK solicitors** 112
▶ **Inheritance tax** 117
▶ **Names of purchasers** 139

Other sources...
▶ **If you wish to find a lawyer in the UK who can advise on all aspects of French tax and property law, go to:** www.bllaw.co.uk www.nlcc.co.uk
▶ **For more information on French taxes, you can go to the French websites and choose 'translate' if you enter through Google:** www.impots.gouv.fr www.vosdroits.service-public.fr

7 Making an offer

Once you have seen a property you want, the only way forward is to put in an offer. Do not hesitate. Discuss a possible offer with your agent, taking their advice on board, and ask them to contact the owner on your behalf. Your offer can be verbal and the vendor can accept or refuse or come back with a figure that is nearer to your offer. Don't go so low that it will offend the vendor; offer just below what you can afford to pay in euros. New developments are not negotiable; if you see a property you want, you must reserve it immediately.

Putting in an offer

You finally arrive outside a property that looks as though it will fulfil all your dreams! So often this is the moment when you just know that this is going to be the right property for you.

must know

Before making an offer
▶ Check with your agent as to what they suggest you offer. Is it guesswork or have they discussed the price with the owner or had an offer rejected? Has the price been reduced? Is the owner keen to move or has the property just come onto the market?
▶ Check that the asking price includes agency commission.
▶ Check what the *notaire's* fees are likely to be.
▶ State if you prefer a fast or slow completion or are willing to fit in with the owner's timescale.
▶ If you are cash buyers then mention this when putting in your offer – it can sometimes persuade the owner to accept.

The right property

As you walk around the property your excitement rises; it seems to have exactly the layout and type of accommodation that appeals to you. Perhaps not everything is perfect but compromises always have to be made and, in general, it has most of your requirements and is so appealing that you are happy to overlook any minor defects.

You are in no hurry to leave and you would like to see it all again but, on the other hand, you cannot wait to leave so that you can discuss an offer with your agent. It is acceptable in France to make a lower offer on a property but, unlike the UK, the agent will often be in a position to advise you as to how much they believe the owner might accept.

In some cases the agent will just make an educated guess which may, of course, turn out to be wrong. Sometimes they has already discussed the bottom line with the owners and will be able to inform you of the price that they are prepared to take. Strangely enough, in some cases, the agent, thinking that you might be interested in the property and aware of your budget, may negotiate with the owner on your behalf even before you discuss putting in an offer, so that when they tell you what would be acceptable it will be the very best price that you can get.

Deciding on a figure

When deciding on how much to offer, you must take account of the general values of the houses you may have seen in the area. If the property needs some work carried out on it, then it is probable that this has already been taken into account so it is not feasible to expect to be able to deduct what you need to spend on it nor is it reasonable to expect a reduction because you want to enlarge or change it.

Don't assume that a French vendor will think in the same way as a British vendor. If the property has been on the market for some time, then it may be that the vendor has not been keen or helpful about showing it or it may be that it was over-priced originally and is now about right. You may feel that as it has been on the market for a while that the vendor will accept a low offer – that may not be the case. The vendor may not be negotiable and will stick out for the asking price.

There is excitement and pleasure at the agency when your offer for a French property is accepted.

must know

The right price
When you make your offer, bear in mind the property has been priced to take account of any work that may be required and its location will have contributed greatly to how it has been priced. So don't expect when looking at a property that perhaps needs a new kitchen and bathroom, or maybe a lot more, that you can deduct the cost of these works from the asking price – allowances will have already been made. At least you will now have the opportunity to do the work to your personal taste. Likewise if the property is not in the best of positions – if it had been sited more favourably with a sea view it would have been priced higher accordingly.

French negotiations are often a little more straightforward but it is essential that you start with a sensible offer in order to get a response. Having received your offer the vendor will respond with what they will accept, and on many occasions this really will be the bottom line, rather than in the UK where purchasers and vendors go up and down, little by little. Obviously each negotiation is different.

Mortgage considerations

If you are intending to apply for a mortgage on the property in France then this will be a condition of the contract that you will sign and will give you the possibility of pulling out should your application for a mortgage be refused. Hence the vendor will have to wait perhaps two to three months before knowing that the property has definitely been sold.

If a mortgage clause is put into the contract it will make it subject to mortgage. There is usually a limited period of around two months to get a mortgage offer or a refusal from a bank. Once you have your offer it will be confirmed to the *notaire* and the contract becomes unconditional.

What happens if you get a refusal on your mortgage application? It must be a refusal from a bank confirming that they cannot lend you the amount of money you require on the property you wish to buy. If you are not able to proceed to purchase then this letter must then be sent with a letter of retraction from you by recorded delivery to the *notaire* within the period given on the contract. The *notaire* will then be in a position to refund your deposit to you.

If you have a mortgage clause you don't necessarily have to apply for a mortgage; the contract will become unconditional after the given period of time. If you get a refusal of mortgage after the expiry of the condition, it will be too late to get your deposit back.

If you don't have a mortgage clause in the contract, either because you did not intend taking out a mortgage or because the vendor would not accept it, it does not prevent you from applying and taking a mortgage of which the *notaire* will then be informed.

Note that if you are taking out a loan on your property in the UK or any other than the property you are purchasing then the conditional mortgage clause cannot be inserted into the contract.

If you do not require the mortgage clause, you will be required to write a paragraph declaring this in French on the contract and then sign it. As stated, it does not prevent you from getting a mortgage; it is just that the contract is not conditional on it.

must know

Surveys
Although you may want to have the property surveyed, a survey cannot normally be made a condition of the contract. You will need to arrange to have this carried out speedily so that you have the result prior to the expiry of your seven-day cooling-off period.

Other conditions

State any further conditions that you might want to apply to your offer, such as timing for completion, permission for a pool, etc. For instance, if you are made aware that the owners would like the use of their property for the next four months and this is not a problem to you, then you might find them more amenable to a lower offer if you can offer them this possibility.

It may be a good idea to have a survey carried out on an older property, but you will have to do this quickly.

The *compromis*

Under French law if the vendor accepts your offer, whether it is verbal or written, then an agreement is reached and this is binding on both parties, although in reality it would be almost impossible to hold you to a verbal agreement.

The initial contract

Normal practice is that an offer is made to which the vendor will respond. Once an agreement has been reached the agent or *notaire* will draw up a *compromis* which includes your personal details, details of the property you are purchasing, the price, costs and the timescale – the date by which any conditions have to be met and a final date for the signing. This date on the contract, unlike a UK contract, is the one by which completion should take place, not the actual day that it will take place.

> **must know**
>
> **Copies**
> Take copies of your personal documents with you if you are serious about buying a house. It is helpful to speak to your bank prior to your visit to arrange for them to take your instructions by fax or phone to transfer a deposit – just in case you find yourself in a position where sending your deposit might secure the property.

The *état civil*

Once your offer is accepted the agent will ask you to complete an *état civil*. This is just a sheet of personal information which is required to be put into the contract. The information requested will be as follows:

▶ Your full name, including maiden name if applicable.

▶ Your address and telephone numbers.

▶ The date and place of your birth.

▶ The date and place of your marriage – it will ask what type of marriage contract you have but you can write 'not applicable' as we do not have choices in the UK.

▶ The date and place of divorce if applicable.

▶ A copy of your passport, birth and marriage certificates will be required but if you don't have them to hand then you can post these at a later date.

The cooling-off period

Both you, as the purchaser, and the owner will be required to sign the contract and it will then be passed to the *notaire* to carry out their work on the sale in order to conclude the conveyance of the property. The *notaire* or the agent will issue a letter giving you notice of a seven-day cooling-off period (seven working days). During this period you can retract from the sale without any valid reason. If this is the case, you will need to send a recorded delivery letter to the *notaire* or agent, whoever sent you the notification in the first place, within this period in order to retract.

The deposit

A deposit of 10 per cent is normally required on a resale property, although it is sometimes possible to negotiate a five per cent deposit on larger properties. On new properties a deposit of between two and five per cent is required. You will need to transfer these funds to the *notaire's* account which is a client account. Occasionally you may be asked to pay the money to the agent's client account and this is quite normal. *Notaires* cannot accept cash as a deposit. Therefore you can pay by cheque if you have a French account, or you can transfer monies from your French or UK account.

Don't delay

You should be aware that until you enter into negotiations for a property it can be sold at any time, so if you are determined to buy you cannot afford to 'play it cool' and leave it a day or two. Unlike the UK where the exchange of contracts can take weeks or months, it is possible for a purchaser to view a property and sign a contract within an hour. If a vendor knows of your interest they may give you the chance to match an offer.

Taking advice

You may wish to take advice on your contract either before signing or during your seven-day cooling-off period. Make sure that you go to a well-recommended solicitor, and check that they speak French, that they are qualified in both French and UK law and that they can act quickly for you. Don't hesitate to ask how much they charge prior to instructing them.

must know

UK solicitors
If you intend using a solicitor in the UK it is a good idea to instruct them before you go to France to view and arrange that a copy of any contract can be emailed or faxed to them for their immediate perusal so that you can sign the contract whilst you are in France.

Whether you want to buy a small apartment or a *château*, make sure you use a good solicitor.

A solicitor in the UK will advise you. However, if you have an English speaking *notaire*, or you are French speaking, then remember that your *notaire* is acting for you and although he will not necessarily be pro-active in advising you, he is well qualified to answer any questions you may have.

Clause of substitution

You may need advice on how to buy the property, i.e. in personal names or as a company, etc. If you are not sure what names you may want to use at the point of signing then make sure there is a 'clause of substitution' in the contract – this will allow you to change the names of the purchasers in the final completion contract.

Waiting to complete

During this time you are unlikely to hear anything from the *notaire*. If you are applying for a mortgage you will need to apply immediately. You should make use of this time to find out about how the inheritance laws will affect your personal situation and make arrangements accordingly.

If your vendor is accommodating, you may be able to obtain estimates for any works you would like to do, and measure up and order any furniture or fittings so that they are ready for completion.

This would be many people's dream property – a restored stone house with a private pool in a secluded location. You still have seven days to change your mind even if you get carried away!

New properties

When purchasing new properties, there is no negotiation; the properties are sold at the prices stated. It is often possible to take an option on a property several days prior to viewing in order to be sure that it remains available for you but there is no obligation to proceed.

must know

Becoming the owner
It is at the point of the *ouverture de chantier* or *achèvement des fondations* that you become the owner of the property and sign the *acte de vente* at the *notaire's* office. It is not necessary to insure the property as the builder will have it insured until the time of building completion. Although you will be completing on the property when you sign the *acte de vente*, the property is not completed, i.e. not finished and ready to be handed over.

Buying off-plan

Once you have viewed the site you can confirm your reservation or withdraw. A reservation contract will be drawn up once you confirm your interest. As mentioned earlier in the book, new properties are generally purchased off-plan and completion dates for completion of the building can be anything from six months to as much as two years after you have signed your reservation contract.

However, you will need to make your mortgage application immediately, regardless of the timing of the purchase, as you will be given a limited time for this to be approved or refused.

Stage payments

You will pay for an off-plan property in a series of stage payments. Each contract will vary slightly in the exact amounts and timing of these payments but they will be approximately as follows:

- *Dépôt de garantie* (deposit): five per cent.
- *Ouverture de chantier* (works start): 25 per cent.
- *Achèvement des fondations* (foundations laid): five per cent.
- *Plancher bas rez-de-chaussée* (ground floor stage): 30 per cent.
- *Mise hors d'eau* (roof on): five per cent.

▶ *Menuiserie extérieures posées* (second fixing): 20 per cent.

▶ *Achèvement des travaux* (works completed): five per cent.

▶ *Remise des clés* (handing over of the keys after snagging is completed): five per cent.

Buying new

With all new developments you will have to wait for them to be completed: a few months, a year or even longer, but by paying today's prices, when you take possession of your property it should be worth more than you paid for it. Buying new helps in making friends with other people in the development and improving your French. New houses can prove to be a good investment as well as offering you a trouble-free holiday home if you are prepared to wait for it to be built.

must know

Mortgage payments
If you are taking a mortgage, the lending company will continue the payments after you have paid your contribution. They will ask permission each time before handing over the money.

When you buy a new off-plan property, you may well only be able to see an artist's impression of what the finished development will look like.

The *notaire*

A *notaire* is a legally qualified person who is a member of a highly respected profession. *Notaires* deal with all matters relating to family and property law in France and they are also empowered to collect taxes where applicable.

must know

Using the same *notaire*
As both you and the vendor want the same thing, using the same *notaire* will achieve this more easily. *Notaires* are not biased and will act in your best interests; their job is to complete the conveyance correctly for both parties.

Choosing a *notaire*

It is usual for a *notaire* to act for both the purchaser and vendor in a property sale and that the purchaser pays the costs. The *notaire* is appointed to ensure that the transaction is completed in accordance with French law. They will act on behalf of both parties and are therefore not committed to protecting your sole interest but will advise you on any subject pertaining to the purchase if asked. You can choose your *notaire* but it is advisable to go to one in the area in which you are buying a property, preferably one with whom your agent has a good rapport. Your agent will usually recommend a *notaire* to you and will liaise with them throughout the purchase procedure. It is inadvisable to use a *notaire* from a different area as this often causes delays. If you do use two separate *notaires* there are no extra fees to pay – they are forced to accept half each of the normal fee. Always remember that a *notaire* is addressed as *Maître*, whether male or female.

The *notaire's* duties

The *notaire* will do the local searches, check the ownership of the property and ensure that there are no outstanding loans on the property, etc. You can arrange to meet up to discuss in what name to purchase the property. The reason for concern about this is the French inheritance tax laws which vary from those in the UK and will apply to you even if you remain a UK tax payer and live in the UK.

Inheritance tax

You can also talk to the *notaire* about inheritance tax issues. In France you are forced by the inheritance tax laws to leave your property to your children. For many people this presents no problem, but if you are a couple on your second marriage and one or both of you have children from your first marriage this can be complicated.

If you buy the property 50:50 between you and you have two children who both belong to you, on the first death they will inherit 33 per cent each of the 50 per cent and the spouse will get the remaining 33 per cent. They could insist on the sale of the property to realize this.

If you buy the property 50:50 between you and you both have two children from earlier marriages, on your death your children will receive one-third each of your 50 per cent and your spouse will receive up to one-third. So in effect your spouse will then own approximately 66.6 per cent of the property and your children will own the other 33.4 per cent. Your spouse will end up owning it with your children and his/her children will not receive anything until the second death when they will share

When you are buying a property in France, no matter how large or small, you must consider inheritance tax implications.

7 Making an offer

Tips on buying

► Speak French – or start learning – it will enhance your enjoyment of your property and France in general.

► Measure a room in your house to see how many square metres it makes to give you a better feel for the details that you receive on French properties; if they have room measurements they will normally be in square metres.

► Use the same common sense that you would apply when doing any transaction.

► Researching different areas and properties in advance can be useful – but there is no substitute for going and seeing the properties 'in the flesh' and hearing all the details from the local agency as to how things work in that area – things can vary slightly from region to region. It is better to believe what you are told 'on the ground' than the intricate details supplied in books as laws and procedures do change.

► When in France do as the French do; don't try to change the rules or do things in a different way and don't make the process harder than it needs to be. Stay within the normal framework of how business is carried out in France, and don't try to make it work as it does in the UK.

► Use local people for surveys, legal advice and estimates for work – they know the area, the prices and the properties.

► Make sure you are dealing with a registered French agent in France – or that your UK-based agent only deals with registered agents. The status of the French agent is different to that in the UK – never buy from someone whom you meet in a café who has a friend with a property to sell.

► Enjoy the process – make sure you understand what is going on and why so that the procedure can be as stress-free as possible.

► You have to trust someone sometime – once you have chosen who to deal with, stay with them. Don't ask all and sundry to check what they are saying.

► Try and buy with an estate agent you are comfortable with so that you can ask them for help at any time and feel they have your best interests at heart.

► Make househunting fun and exciting – if a house doesn't excite you, maybe you are not buying the right property.

► Don't lose a property just because of a small amount of money – if the vendor won't accept your offer, try to get the extra money together. A temporary small loan in the UK or a mortgage on the French property is all it takes; within a few years you won't even notice the extra you have paid.

► Follow French etiquette, but don't get upset if they don't do as we would do – it is their country.

► If you have a complicated family set-up, make sure you get advice as to the best names to purchase the property in.

► If you are intending to get work done on your property after purchase make sure that you comply with the regulations regarding how much you can build, i.e. how many square metres, how high you can build and what changes you are allowed to make to the exterior, etc.

► For any changes that affect the structure of your property, make sure you use registered builders who are able to give a 10-year guarantee to protect your investment.

the 66.6 per cent between the two of them – i.e. they will get the lion's share.

Couples who are living together but are unmarried are not recognized as a unit so if there are no children your share would go to another member of your family, ie. your father, mother, niece, etc.

Dealing with inheritance tax

You can change your marriage contract – the *notaire* will do this for you. It is simply a matter of signing a form but it will allow the property to be passed to the remaining spouse in its entirety on the first death, i.e. it will work more or less exactly as it would in the UK. Alternatively, you can buy it in such a way as to give the remaining spouse the right to keep the house during their lifetime.

You can buy in the name of a company – either a UK company or a French property holding company called an SCI (*Société Civile Immobilière*). The *notaire* will be able to do this for you for an extra charge. Buying in the name of a company will take you out of the family law rules for inheritance so that you can leave the shares in these companies to whoever you wish.

However, you should also be aware that there can be other tax implications associated with these companies and you should take advice on both the French and UK tax situation from a solicitor who is qualified both in the UK and France so that they understand the effects in both countries.

You can, of course, make a will and then leave the property to whoever you want, but if you leave it to other family members or friends the taxes will be higher.

want to know more?

Take it to the next level...

- Getting a mortgage 78
- Buying euros 82
- Maintenance charges 94

Other sources...

- Although you will normally choose a local *notaire* who is recommended by the agent with whom you are dealing, you can go to the *Chambre des Notaires* official website at: www.cdnq.org
- To find a qualified bi-lingual lawyer, see: www.bllaw.co.uk www.nlcc.co.uk
- To start learning French from scratch or to improve your conversation and language skills, see: www.bbc.co.uk/languages/French www.linkwordlanguages.com/French
- Look in your local bookshop at the selection of French language phrase books, dictionaries and instruction books and language tapes and courses (see page 189)

8 Solving potential problems

The property conveyancing law in France is very protective of a purchaser, so if you abide by the rules you will not experience any problems or loss of money. Hopefully, with the information in this book to hand, you will have a better understanding of the French system and will be making the correct decisions as to how to go about your purchase. On rare occasions, even after signing a first contract and sending your deposit, it may not be possible for you to buy the property, but should this occur you will always get your money back.

Pre-emption rights

Should any of the examples below apply either to the property you are buying or to your vendor, it is possible that your purchase could be pre-empted, although this happens extremely rarely.

Droit de pré-emption

I have seen this happen only twice: once when a *commune* needed a house for its own use – in this case the purchaser got his deposit back; and the other occasion when a property had so much land that the SAFER (see opposite) insisted that it continued to be farmed. Luckily the purchaser had farming qualifications, was accepted and could buy the property.

In France when a seller disposes of their property it is vital to understand that certain authorities have the right to purchase the property in priority to the proposed purchaser. This is called the *droit de pré-emption*. There are four ways in which this right of pre-emption may be exercised. These are as follows:

It is extremely rare for a property to be subject to the right of pre-emption.

Right of the *commune*

The first right of pre-emption is the right of the *commune* where the property is situated. This right is known as the *droit de pré-emption urbain* (DPU). The *Mairie's* office usually exercises the right where the property or land is required for development purposes, including public works, leisure facilities, etc. The DPU starts by a notification called a *déclaration d'intention d'aliéner* (DIA) which is sent to the *Mairie* who have two months within which to reply. The DIA is usually drawn up by the *notaire* who is in charge of the sale of the property concerned. If the Mairie does not intend to *pré-empter* it can either not reply or it can send the DIA back with the comment '*droit non exercé*' (right not exercised) or '*droit n'existe pas*' (right does not exist).

Where the *Mairie* does exercise its pre-emption right it usually purchases the property at a lower price than the purchase price which is indicated in the DIA. In these circumstances, the seller has three options:

▶ To withdraw from the sale and keep the property.

▶ To accept the *Mairie's* offer at the lower price.

▶ To maintain the asking price and then let a judge fix the price at which the *Mairie* purchases the property.

Tenant of a property

The second right of pre-emption can be exercised by the tenant of a property but these are extremely rare occurrences. In this case, there are two rights of pre-emption. When an owner decides to sell a property occupied by a tenant the landlord must send a notification to the tenant who has one month within which to reply. Where he wishes to buy the property, he has two months to complete the purchase or four months if the tenant requires a loan.

Importantly both the relevant laws of 1975 and 1989 provide security for the tenant if the landlord sells the property without notifying them or sells it at a lower price. The tenant can challenge the sale and, within one month following completion, take priority over the purchaser.

Rural areas

The third right of pre-emption is in relation to rural areas. The farmer and the *Société d'Aménagement Foncier et d'Etablissement Rural* (SAFER or, in English, the Agricultural Commission) both have a right of pre-emption over land or property.

If you are buying a property with more than half a hectare (1.2 acres) of land, it has to be offered to the SAFER. They exist to protect agricultural land and its continued use, so a property with a few acres is not really of interest to them but the law says they must be informed. The notification is sent to them by letter and from receipt they have two months in which to reply after which the sale can proceed if they decide not to purchase. However, if SAFER intends to

Old properties in rural areas may occasionally, albeit rarely, be subject to a *droit de pré-emption*.

purchase the property the same rules will apply as to the *droit de pré-emption urbain*, and notification of the *droit de pré-emption* is published in a newspaper.

Farmers may purchase the agricultural land where they effectively use the land; have worked as farmers on the land for three years; the total surface of the land they use is over 1 hectare (2.5 acres); the land they own has a total surface area of less than the *surface minimum d'insertion*; or they commit themselves to using the land continuously for nine years.

Joint property

The fourth right is exercised by the *coindivisaire* and this relates to joint property. If one of them sells his/her share then the other *indivisaires* may purchase the share. The seller serves a letter by a *huissier de justice* on the other *indivisaires* and they then have one month within which to answer it. If the other *indivisaires* wish to purchase the share they must do so within a time limit of two months.

The consequences of the *droit de pré-emption* are that the potential purchaser is obliged to let the *pre-empteur* buy the property and they will recover all the deposits made to the estate agent or *notaire*.

No rights to purchase

Finally, there are some properties that the *Mairie*, a tenant or a farmer cannot purchase because they do not have a *droit de pré-emption*. These circumstances are where:

1 The *Mairie* cannot exercise its right for sale of *lots de copropriété* if the *règlement de copropriété* has been registered for more than 10 years, or if the sale of the property has been completed more than 10 years ago, or if the property is to be built in the future (*vente à terme et vente en l'état futur d'achèvement*).

2 A farmer cannot pre-empt a sale taking place between the members of the family until the *troisième degré*, which means the nieces, nephews and uncles.

3 The tenant cannot pre-empt a sale taking place between the members of the family until the *quatrième degré*, which means cousins under the Law of 31 December 1975, and the *troisième degré*.

Problems of your own making

It has to be said that all the following scenarios happen only very rarely and, on many occasions, deposits are returned even when they don't have to be. However, you should be aware of them.

must know

Reports
▶ In most areas, the vendor is required to provide reports on lead (only in paintwork) asbestos and termites by the completion date but not required to act on the reports. Should any of these be found in huge quantities you may have the right to withdraw. The vendor must provide these reports but does not have to deal with any problems. However, most vendors will get them treated or removed , or they may ask that the costs are shared with the purchaser.
▶ The *notaire* will do searches on the property to confirm ownership, that it is free of debts and local searches. If anything untoward is discovered you have the right to withdraw.
▶ If the owner dies between the first and second contracts, this can elongate the process and you may experience a delay.

Mortgages

If you apply for a mortgage outside of the time frame given in the *compromis* and your application is refused after the contract has become unconditional, the vendor can refuse to return your deposit.

Currency fluctuations

If the euro/sterling exchange rate changes dramatically you may find that your sterling will not buy you enough euros. Don't leave it until the last minute to purchase the euros – agree the rate and purchase at the time of agreeing the price unless you want to gamble on the actual cost of your property – of course, the exchange rate could improve.

Delays

If you delay in returning the signed contract and sending your deposit, then the vendor may sell elsewhere. If you need a little more time to deal with the contract, keep everyone informed. You must realize that the normal time scale in France is much shorter than in the UK for this first signing, so you should possibly send your deposit to secure the property meanwhile.

Deposits and contracts

A *notaire* cannot keep a deposit for any length of time if they do not have a signed contract to go with it – so it could be returned before you send the contract. If you sign a contract but don't send a deposit, the *notaire* will require a letter by recorded delivery to release you from the contract.

Delay in signing the final contract

On the *compromis*, the final date by which you can sign is noted. However, an earlier date can be fixed once the *notaire* has finished work. If, due to reasons of your own making, you are unable or unwilling to sign by that date then, in most cases, if you let the agents know they may be able to agree a later date with the vendor of the property.

Don't risk losing your dream property – make sure you deal with everything within the time scale laid down in the *compromis*.

However, at this point the vendor of the property has the right to ask the *notaire* to serve a notice to complete on you. This will give you another 14 days' notice that you must complete. If you are unwilling or unable to complete within this time frame, the law says that you will lose your 10 per cent deposit to the vendor and also the right to buy the property. By the same token, however, if the vendor refuses to complete then they will have to return your 10 per cent deposit and pay you an additional 10 per cent as compensation.

You or the vendor can take this further if you feel that you are out of pocket by more than this and require compensation – but in 17 years of selling property in France I have never seen this happen. In fact, in the one or two cases where purchasers have not completed they have only lost their deposit after a period of several months has elapsed.

Scenario

Try to put yourself in a French vendor's position. A 'foreigner' who speaks no French agrees to buy your property and then goes back to the UK promising to sign a contract and send a deposit. Two weeks later you've heard nothing, probably because the purchaser is getting everything checked out by their solicitor. In the meantime, a French purchaser views the property with another agency, agrees to buy, and offers to go back to the agency, sign the contract and give the agent a French cheque for the deposit. What would you do?

Utilities

Make sure you ask whether water and electricity are connected. If they have just been disconnected, it costs very little to organize re-connection. However, if the property has never been connected, check how far away the source is. It could be just at the boundary, which will mean that the cost of connection will be low, but if it is at the end of the street, or several kilometres away, you could be asked to pay for it to be brought to the property. If this is the case, you must get an estimate for this prior to signing your *compromis* (first contract) or make it a condition of the contract so that if it costs over a certain amount, you are able to withdraw.

Swimming pools

In most regions of France planning permission for a swimming pool is not required, but it is worth checking with the *Mairie* before proceeding to purchase a property that you may put in a pool if that is what you intend doing. There may be restrictions in force in some areas. Your local agent will be able to advise you and will probably accompany you or go for you to the *Mairie*.

Safety regulations

Laws have recently been introduced in France stating that you must install some security measures on your pool to prevent any accidents. You must either have a pool alarm or fencing of a certain height around the pool which complies with the regulations. After January 2006 these regulations will be in force for all pools, private and public, so if you are purchasing a property with a pool you should check that it complies with the law. If you are having a pool built, it will be the responsibility of the pool company to advise you on what is necessary.

Taking pets to France

The Pet Travel Scheme (PETS) now includes more than 50 countries worldwide. Over half the 40,000 cats and dogs that have used the scheme have been British-registered pets going to and from France. However, even now there is still some unnecessary confusion among owners, despite all the information being so readily available from vets and the Department for Environment, Food & Rural Affairs (DEFRA, formerly MAFF).

DEFRA's procedures are designed to keep Britain free of rabies and other animal-borne diseases, and new users of the PETS scheme will find it smooth sailing as long as they understand how and why it operates, and then remember to plan well ahead of their journey to France, because, in order to avoid quarantine, your dog or cat must be vaccinated against rabies at least seven months in advance of its re-entry into the UK.

Before you travel to France

Your pet first needs to be microchipped and, at the same time, or later, can be vaccinated against rabies — providing that it is more than three months old. Thirty days after the injection is the optimum time for a blood test to be taken, and once an approved laboratory has checked that the vaccine has taken successfully your vet can issue you with a PETS Re-entry Certificate (PETS 1). This document links the pet's unique microchip number to both the vaccination and the successful

If you are buying a holiday home in France and intend to take your pets with you, then check out the Pet Passport procedure with your vet well in advance.

blood test, and once this has been confirmed you can take your dog or cat out of the UK whenever you want. But the animal cannot use this certificate to re-enter Britain until six months after the successful blood test. The return journey back to the UK need not cause difficulty either, as long as you are mindful of DEFRA's requirements.

There are still a significant number of failed or, at least, delayed re-entries to Britain when pet owners check in for their return journey. Ninety-eight per cent of failures result from the mistiming of the tick and worm treatment (see below). Either pet owners or the French vets do not fully understand the system and they turn up too early or too late to travel.

Re-entry procedure

Before re-entering Britain your pet must be treated against certain ticks as well as a tapeworm that can be carried by cats and dogs. The French vet must also use a scanner to check that your PETS certificate applies to the microchip number of the animal being examined and treated.

An individually numbered official French government certificate must be signed and stamped to not only confirm the pet's vaccination details, as shown on your PETS certificate, but also must give the date and specific time that the tick and worm treatments were administered. The timing of this treatment is crucial to your pet's successful re-entry.

Your pet will only be allowed to check in with an approved transport company for its journey back into Britain between 24 and 48 hours after these treatments are administered. This is so that after the tapeworm treatment your pet has time to excrete any remaining live worms on French soil, not Britain's! At the port of departure the DEFRA and French documents will be checked, and a scanner will be used to confirm that all the papers do indeed relate to the micro-chipped pet which is about to enter Britain.

must know

Resident French pets
If your dog or cat resides in France then similar PETS procedures apply for entering the UK. Check with DEFRA for variations and the latest requirements, plus information for your French vet.

The pet's owner also has to sign a declaration of residency (PETS 3) confirming that the pet has not been outside any of the qualifying countries for six months. This simple procedure takes place as you check in for the ferry or shuttle and, if everything is in order, it takes only a few minutes just before you drive on board.

Tick treatment
Responsible pet owners will regularly administer an anti-tick treatment to their cats or dogs, especially while they are in France because of the greater risk there of certain parasite-related illnesses. However, such treatment by the owner is voluntary and thus it cannot be proved to have taken place. Hence

Even if you live full-time in France, it is still a good idea to have Pet Passports for your pets in case you return to the UK with them.

DEFRA requires the French vet to apply an approved treatment for ticks – usually Frontline – at this vital pre-departure appointment. For more information on this, go to the DEFRA website (see page 189).

Finding a vet

The French vets who are situated closest to the Channel ports were the first to become familiar with the PETS procedures, but now pet-owning British property-owners all over France can locate local vets who are able to carry out the required treatment.

Help is at hand! *Les Pages Jaunes* (French *Yellow Pages*) can be accessed via DEFRA's excellent website (see page 189) and then searched (in English or in French) to locate the vets who are most convenient to where you would like to have your animal treated. There are also useful French phrases for using when dealing with a vet. It's a good idea to print these off and keep them handy.

Which route?

DEFRA will advise you of all approved routes and carriers, including airlines. The Eurotunnel shuttle is the most popular carrier because owners can remain in their car with their pets and it is the shortest crossing. On any ferry trip the pet must remain unaccompanied in your vehicle on the car deck, although on longer crossings you should be able to check on it with a member of the crew.

want to know more?

Take it to the next level...

► **Currency fluctuations** 82
► **Purchase procedure** 110
► **Utilities** 142, 148

Other sources...

► **For information on how to obtain a Pet Passport, talk to your vet and look on the DEFRA website:**
www.defra.gov.uk/animal h/quarantine
► **For assistance with taking your dog(s) to France, see:**
www.dogsaway.co.uk
► **To find out more about swimming pool safety laws:**
www.riviera.angloinfo.com
► **For contact information on travelling by air, rail or ferry to France, see page 188.**

9 Signing the final contract

The signing of the final *acte de vente* at the *notaire's* office can be an enjoyable occasion, particularly if you have had a good relationship with your vendors. After the meeting you will be the proud owners of a property in France and can move straight in. As mentioned earlier, when a vendor wants to sell and a purchaser wants to buy you are both working to achieve the same end – the French perception is that you are both on the 'same side' unlike the UK where solicitors sometimes seem at war with each other during the conveyancing process.

Attending the signing

All signatories to the contract must attend the *notaire's* office. The *notaire* must be certain that you understand the contract you are going to sign, and may insist on a translator being present. If this is the case, the cost of the translator is payable by you.

must know

Mortgage offer
When you receive a French mortgage offer the law states you must wait 11 days before signing and returning the offer to accept the mortgage – this is a cooling-off period so you don't make a hasty decision. You need to allow for this time in your planning of the appointment for signature.

Preparing for the signing

When the *notaire's* work is complete, you or your agent will normally be informed that they are ready to sign the *acte de vente* whenever a convenient date can be agreed. You will need to give your agent a date that would be possible for you and they will liaise with your vendor and *notaire* to find a mutually convenient date.

By this time you will need to have received your mortgage offer and accepted it so that the *notaire* has been notified that the funds are available. The *notaire* will then be able to call for the funds once the date is fixed – they will normally take about a week to come through. It is essential that your personal funds are in the *notaire's* account as cleared funds on the day of completion as they will have to write a cheque or make a transfer to the owner's account on the day of completion. If these funds are not there on the day, you cannot complete. Apart from being a nuisance to you as you will not be able to take possession, it may mean that the vendors cannot complete on their next purchase without the funds.

Although UK banks state that funds will be transferred within 48 hours using the SWIFT or BACS system, there can be a delay in France as the money is often sent first to Paris or the head office of the area and then onto the *notaire's* account. If possible, you should allow 15 days for the money to get there to save any disappointment – it is better to be safe than sorry.

Visiting the property

It is advisable to visit the property in the morning or the day before the signing to confirm that it has not deteriorated in any way and that all is as it should be. It will also be useful if your vendor can show you how the house 'works': the heating and boiler, the plumbing and where the stop cock is to be found, how the locks work, if there is an alarm or a safe, etc. You will also need to know the contact numbers for the repair and maintenance people and whether there are manuals for any machines that are being left behind in the house. If you are lucky, you may also be given the names of doctors, dentists and vets and even the vendor's recommendations for the best local butchers and bakers. You might also 'inherit' their cleaner or gardener which can be a great help as they will already be familiar with the property and will have proved to be trustworthy to your vendor.

must know

Termite surveys
These have to be done within three months of completion, so do not ask your vendor to do one immediately if you are not completing for several months as this would mean he would need to have another one carried out near to completion.

It is really important to maintain a good relationship with your vendor if you possibly can. Bear in mind that you will be left in charge of a property in a foreign country and your vendor's good will may well save you a lot of heartache when it comes to the small but inevitable problems that may arise – the heating may not come on, the key will not open a certain door or who do you call if you want more firewood delivered, etc. Which day does the dustman come, where do you put your bin to be emptied, and are there any local rules regarding recycling?

The act of signing

When the big moment finally arrives for the signing, the *notaire* will invite you all into his or her office and read the contract aloud, stopping to explain anything that they may feel needs an explanation, with the translator (if present) translating throughout. Feel free to ask any questions as to the meaning and implications of the laws and statements in the contract. The size of the property, number of rooms, area of the land and address, etc. are stated to confirm that you are purchasing the correct property and that its description complies with the original contract.

Check your property with the vendor or agent before you go to the signing; make sure you know how everything works within the property.

Surveys

The *notaire* will go through the surveys that have been provided by the vendor of the property in order to confirm that they are in order and also to let you know whether any works may be necessary. Usually if the reports provided indicate a problem, then you would have been informed of this prior to the meeting to sign the *acte de vente*.

In the event that any of the reports or descriptions differ greatly to your expectations, then they may allow you to withdraw from the purchase of the property, even at this late stage. However, in normal circumstances any problems are sorted out between all the parties concerned to their mutual agreement.

Names of purchasers

By the time of this signing you should have informed the *notaire* of the names in which you want to purchase the property, i.e. company, personal names, etc. It may be that the *notaire* will have prepared a change of marriage contract for you to sign at the same time or will have formed a company (SCI). It is a good idea to check again, even at this stage, that you are buying in the right manner but, hopefully, you will have made sure that you have dealt with this much earlier in the purchase procedure.

Signing in triplicate

Once the contract and reports have been read and approved by both parties, the document is ready to sign. It is normal for some amendments to be made so the *notaire* may have to keep you waiting for a few minutes whilst the contract is prepared in triplicate for you all to sign. The contracts and plans, etc. are then passed along the table like a conveyor belt – with everyone initialling the bottom right-hand corner of each page and finally signing at the end: *lu et approuvé, bon pour achat* and your full name.

The *notaire* will also have to sign to confirm that the conveyance has been done according to the law and the translator to confirm that you have understood everything. When signing any document in France it is usual that you not only sign but that you write in French 'read and approved' and/or 'good to buy' or 'good to sell', etc. This is probably a safety measure so that you do not just sign a document without thinking about what you are doing. This applies even when signing an order for goods.

Your copies

You will be given copies of the *acte*. You can also ask the *notaire* for an *attestation*. This is a letter of confirmation that you have purchased the property. The *notaire* can give you two if you wish – one with the price of the property and one without. This can be useful when getting utilities changed into your name and ordering telephone services to prove your ownership. For this reason it is useful to have one without the price of your property on it as the companies very often take a copy and there is no need for them to know how much you paid.

A special occasion

Make the final ceremony special: after signing, invite the vendors for a glass of champagne or take a bottle along with you to give them. The *notaire* may even ask you to join him in a glass.

must know

Making a will

If you require a will to be made in France, the notaire is the person to ask, as they deal with all things relating to family and property law. They will make a small charge for this. However, if you have already discussed the way in which you are buying the property so that it is in an efficient way relating to inheritance tax, it may not be necessary to have a will as the laws relating to inheritance will produce the result you require without one. You may need to add a codicil to your UK will which will refer to your French will; take advice at the time from your *notaire* or solicitor.

Power of attorney

If for any reason you are unable to attend the final signing in person, it is possible to sign by proxy. You can ask the *notaire* to prepare a power of attorney (*procuration*) and send it to you. You will then need to sign this power of attorney in front of a public notary and return it to the *notaire*. By doing this you are in effect giving someone else the right to sign the final *acte* in your place – normally the power of attorney gives the proxy to the *notaire's* clerk. It is a power of attorney for just this signing and does not give them the right to sign on your behalf for anything other than the contract to purchase this property.

However, do try and attend in person if possible. It really is a great shame to miss the final signing as you will not have the opportunity to meet your *notaire*, perhaps for the first time. There is always the possibility that at some future date you may need their services, perhaps to resell the property or for other matters relating to either family or property law, and it would be useful to have met each other.

Secondly, being present at the signing will give you the chance to ask all the questions you may have relating to your purchase and your rights with regard to this. You can discuss any minor discrepancies between what you have understood you are buying and what the contract says, as well as making sure that all the information and personal details are correct and discussing the property and family law in general. It will also give you the chance to meet with your vendors and perhaps cement a friendship with them if they are remaining in the area – at the very least, don't forget to exchange telephone numbers.

New off-plan property

If you are buying a new off-plan property, then the developers or their representative will attend which gives you an opportunity to ask them anything that you would like to know pertaining to the property and the future proceedings of the purchase. You will be signing the *acte* for a new property at the point at which the building has reached ground level and therefore you will not be taking up occupation at this point although you will be the rightful owner.

For new property off-plan purchase you will first be sent the *projet d'acte*, which is a copy of the contract that you will be signing. This is dispatched once the foundations have been completed and with it will be a request for you to attend the *notaire's* office to sign the *acte* plus details of the *notaire's* bank account and the amount that you are requested to send. You will normally be given a month's notice so that you have time to arrange a visit and organize the money transfer.

It is imperative that you respond to this, and in the event that you cannot make a visit within the given time scale, that you let them know immediately when you could attend or ask that a *procuration* be prepared and sent to you. Occasionally, a small additional charge is made by the *notaire* for doing this.

Notaires can be flexible if they are made aware of the situation early, so do not leave it until the last minute before letting them know that you cannot come until, say, two weeks later. Remember that you have signed a legal document to purchase the property and you must act within the boundaries that are set out at the beginning or you risk losing your deposit and property.

Arranging for utilities

Electricity, water and gas companies will transfer the accounts into your name when the vendor closes their account. The bills will automatically be directed to you, so although you will need to sign up for utilities it is not so urgent as it would be in the UK.

must know

Tanks and cylinders
If you have a gas tank, you can order deliveries by lorry from your supplier. If you don't have a tank, you can buy gas cylinder bottles at a supermarket or garage. When you return your empty bottle to the outlet, you will only be able to purchase a new one of the same type.

Signing up utilities

If the property has not been connected previously, or has been disconnected, perhaps because the vendor moved out and it has stood empty, then it is advisable to visit the utility company's local offices to sign up and make sure that you are reconnected. Note that if you are buying a brand-new property, then it is advisable to sign up on the day or previous day to ensure that you are connected. When you do sign up for the utilities, you can arrange for the bills to be sent to your UK address, if wished, and you can also set up a direct debit arrangement for payment from your French bank account (unless you are living in France permanently). The utility companies will send the bill to the UK approximately two weeks before they take the money out of your French bank account by direct debit.

Tariffs and charges

In France, there are various tariffs for electricity and you can discuss with the utility company which one would be the most economical for you – obviously, it will depend on your usage of the property. If you have central heating running on gas or oil you will have to renew your contract with the companies concerned. Water is charged on a metered basis.

The easiest option is probably to take over the utilities on the same tariff as the vendors, and then once you see how it is working for you and the amount of time you spend in the property, go and discuss other possibilities with the utility company. You may find that the electricity supply to your property is not sufficient to run all the machines and appliances. If this is the case, just contact the electricity company and they will send someone along to boost the supply, although this will increase the standard charge.

Gas

This is available in some parts of France but normally only those that are in reasonably built-up areas. There are two types of gas supply available:

▶ Mains gas (*gaz de ville*) which is supplied by *Gaz de France* (GDF).

▶ Bottled gas (propane or butane) which is widely used for heating and cooking.

If you are in an area with mains gas but do not have a supply, you can apply for a new connection (*raccordement*). Ask GDF for an estimate of the costs, which will vary according to the tariff you choose and the distance your house is from the mains supply. If gas is already connected to the property, before moving in, ask your local GDF office for a new account and arrange for the meter to be read.

As with electricity, there are different tariffs to suit different types of houses and usage, e.g. central heating or cooking. You can ask your local GDF/EDF office for a free consultation. Meters are read once every four to six months. There are two elements to your bill (*facture*), which will arrive every two or three months. Firstly, the standing charge (*abonnement*), which is determined by the power supply installed; secondly, the consumption of cubic metres of gas. TVA (Value Added Tax) is applied on the standing charge and consumption but at different rates. You can pay by direct debit based on estimated usage or by settling each bill with a cheque or RIB payment.

want to know more?

Take it to the next level...

▶ **Mortgages** 78
▶ **Off-plan property** 81, 114
▶ **Transferring funds** 82
▶ *Notaires* 116
▶ **Reports** 126

Other sources...
▶ **For power of attorney, you can go to the French consulate to get an** *apostille*, **which is a certificate affixed to a document in accordance with the 1961 Hague Convention.**
▶ **When an** *apostille* **is required, some legal companies can arrange the signing of a procuration for you. You can email: Notary@johnvenn.co.uk**

10 Taking possession

Now that the signing has taken place and you have the keys to your property, you are the proud owner of a home in France. This should be one of the most exciting days of your life. If you have bought a holiday home, you may feel proud that you have amassed the funds for its purchase whereas if it is a permanent home then you will have achieved your ambition of living in France. Even if you are buying a new, off-plan property which is not yet ready for occupation, your time will come.

Inspecting your new property

Most purchasers will hot-foot it round to their new acquisition. It is a strange feeling to let yourself into what was until an hour or so ago someone else's house, even more so because it is in a 'foreign' country, but you will soon make it your own.

must know

Empty houses
If your house is going to be uninhabited for periods of time leave the heating on at a low temperature or drain the water so that you avoid frozen pipes and floods. If you are using your property as a weekend retreat, i.e. often but for short periods, and particularly if it is in northern France, you will find it much more comfortable if you can leave the heating on very low as you will be able to reheat it to a comfortable temperature more quickly. Old houses left without heating in the colder months can take some time to warm up, and if you are going to enjoy your property then you need it to be comfortable.

Location is all important - you can make lots of changes to the property over the coming years but the location will stay the same.

Look around you

As you walk around your new property, you are bound to notice some things that had gone unseen before on previous visits – some good and some not so good. It may be that the feeling of excitement begins to abate as the enormity of what you have done starts to sink in.

The property perhaps does not look quite as lovely when all the pictures have been removed, leaving marks and hooks on the walls; the furniture that looked so right in its setting now leaves a bare room without the ambience you remember. It can be just a bit scary at this point. You may even wonder whether you have made the right decision. However, now is not the time for worrying; take yourself out for a superb meal with wonderful wine and start enjoying the French lifestyle – tomorrow is the first day of your new life.

Keys

It may be advisable to think about changing the locks on your property or perhaps to add an extra one. It will obviously depend on you and how you feel about the vendors. It is just a safety precaution as you cannot be sure about who they may have given keys to in the past.

must know

Broadband
If broadband is
important to you
then check its
availability before
proceeding to
purchase. France
Telecom provide
a 'WIFI digibox'
with simple
instructions to
enable you to
connect your PC
or laptop and
work wireless,
i.e. without wires
plugged in to the
telephone line.

Insurance

You will need to have arranged insurance for your new property. If you are buying in a development or apartment block then normally the insurance will be part of the maintenance and service costs and you should check that it has been put into your name whilst you are at the *notaire's* office.

You will also need to arrange for the cover of your contents. Your estate agent will often be able to arrange this for you and the cost will depend not only on the value of your contents and all-risks belongings but also the area of France. You can arrange this through a UK company if you prefer; there are also some currency transfer companies that offer this service. This does not have to be put in place until you complete on your property, unlike the UK where you are responsible for insuring it from exchange of contracts. On new properties the builder will keep it insured until the day of handing the completed property and keys over to you, rather than at the time of signing the *acte*.

Utilities

The utility companies, i.e. electricity, water and, sometimes, gas, will have your name as the vendors will have notified them when closing their account. That will suffice in the short term and, if wished, you can wait for your first bill to be delivered and then instruct the companies to send your bills to the UK thereafter, if that is what you prefer, and give them a direct debit mandate so that monies are taken from your French account approximately two weeks after you receive your bill.

You may have to make arrangements with oil or *gaz* delivery companies, if your property uses these as fuel. Your vendor will have had a contract with them which can be passed over to you. You will need to contact the company to arrange the details as well as further deliveries. If your heating relies on these fuels, immediately on or just before completion check how much is left and make sure that a delivery is booked before you run out.

If you have a fireplace you will need to find out where to go to buy wood or how to have it delivered. The measurement for purchasing firewood is called a 'step', which equates to 11 large crates. If you have the space where it can just be dumped, then delivery is normally free. If you need it stacked, then there will be a charge.

Telephones

You will need to visit a France Telecom shop to arrange for a land line to be connected. You cannot take over the number of the vendor as in the UK. France Telecom will arrange for an engineer to come to your property to connect your telephone. In my own experience, they have been extremely efficient and arrive on time. You may also require a broadband or ADSL line, which you can arrange with them as long as you are in an area where these services are available.

You may feel that a land line is not necessary in a holiday home and prefer to have only a mobile. Using your UK mobile abroad can prove extremely expensive as you are not only paying reasonably high charges to make phone calls whether the calls are local or back to the UK, but you are also paying each time anyone phones you, again either from around the corner or the UK. When a person calls a UK mobile phone they are charged for the call to that phone as if it was in the UK. As they are not to know where the receiver is, it would not be fair to charge them more than the normal mobile call cost and therefore you have to pick up the tab for the extra cost. It is thus a good idea to have a French mobile phone if you do not have a land line – unless you really want to be isolated from the world.

It is easy enough to purchase a 'pay as you go' phone but calls are slightly more expensive than a phone for which the calls are billed to you each month. To buy a mobile phone with an agreed tariff you will need to show the company a French cheque book and two utility bills for your property and set up a direct debit to your French bank account. The *attestation* from the *notaire* saying that you are the owner of the property may save the wait for utility bills – make sure to show them the one without the price!

General information on your property

If possible, ask your vendor to make a list of contact names, addresses and telephone numbers for all the various workmen, artisans, plumber, electrician, appliance repair men, utilities, etc. Take lots of copies so that you do not lose it – this sheet of paper can be a life line.

If you have been left appliances, then ask for the manuals – even in French they will be better than nothing. In many cases where the product is available internationally, you will be able to phone to request a copy of a manual in English. If you have a benevolent vendor, ask for recommendations of doctors and dentists to put on the list, especially any who can speak some English.

Emergency numbers

There are important numbers for the emergency services in France. You can call these numbers free of charge from home or a public payphone. If you are dialling from a mobile phone, you should dial the Single European emergency call number of 112. Make sure you know the following emergency numbers; it is a good idea to print out this list and keep it by your telephone.

▶ Medical – SAMU: 15 (emergency ambulance for serious medical problems and accidents with injuries).

▶ Police – *Gendarmes*: 17.

▶ Fire – *Pompiers*: 18 (they also deal with other emergencies and rescue situations that they would not deal with in the UK).

▶ Sea or lake rescue: 1616.

▶ Child abuse hotline: 119.

▶ Homeless hotline: 115.

▶ Drugs and alcohol hotline: 113.

Note: European citizens can also dial 112 from a mobile for all the emergency services in all Member States, and you will be directed to the service you require.

Whether you have bought a cottage or a *château*, you may feel overwhelmed with the responsibility when you first let yourself into your new home.

Moving in

If you are making a permanent move to France, it may be that you will want to move all your belongings, including the furniture and electrical equipment, from your home in the UK.

must know

The best time to move in
It is really not a good idea to arrange delivery of furniture or your own goods on the day of completion. You will be tied up with the *notaire* for some of the time so that even if you have a morning appointment the earliest time for delivery will be after lunch and you may prefer to prepare the house ready for its arrival – cleaning, deciding where to put things, etc. It is far better to spend one more night in a local hotel and start work the following morning.

Removal companies

Several removal companies specialize in international moves and they can also store your goods until you take possession of your new French home. It is worth getting two or three estimates and meeting the company representatives to discuss this.

▶ Check carefully that they are quoting for the same service and do take into consideration their general attitude and efficiency and not just the price.

▶ Be sure to check that your goods will be covered by insurance during storage and the move.

If you are buying a second home you may have some furniture that you have no need for in the UK but would like to use in France. Most removal companies will be able to arrange for part-loads to be transported; again, costs and service may vary considerably so contact more than one company.

Be prepared

Try to arrange all this in plenty of time, perhaps as soon as you have signed the first contract even though you may not be sure of the final moving date. You may have a lot to do at the last minute when you are preparing to go to France to sign. It is a good idea to decide on which company you will use so that all you have to do is telephone your chosen company to give them a date. If you are only intending to take small pieces of furniture to France, then you may be able to manage them in your own car by making several journeys.

Furnishing your home

If you don't have the furniture already then why not make your home in France a truly French home? Your lifestyle is going to be different so you may have different needs for which your existing UK furniture may not be suitable. You will find that many goods are cheaper in France, including beds, sofas and kitchen machinery.

Again, it is essential that if you want to be able to move in with some furniture in place you check with the local shops as to delivery times for various items. Although possibly not as long as in the UK, you may have to wait three months for some things. Hopefully, your vendors will have given you access to the house to measure up or to take photos, so you can buy a few of the larger items immediately after signing the first contract in readiness for taking occupation.

must know

Television
It is possible to get UK terrestrial channels and Sky, etc. You can either contact a local television shop in the area of your property or there are some suppliers in the UK that can supply the box to take with you. A DVD and/or video machine may help to make life more interesting, especially if you take possession during the winter months, but the more you listen to French TV the quicker you will learn to speak French. Television and radio are among the best ways to learn a language.

Choosing a style

There are lots of do-it-yourself-type shops dealing with furniture, garden equipment and even soft furnishings. Surely it is more fun to furnish this home in another country in a really different style to the one you have in the UK. It is an opportunity to buy some exciting furniture and accessories – perhaps things that would not suit the character of your British home and the way in which you live. How many times have you looked at pieces of fabric or china and thought how lovely they are but that they would be so unsuitable for the style of your house – now you have the opportunity to experiment.

Holiday homes can still be 'home from homes' although you may choose brighter colours and patterns than you have in the UK.

must know

Restoration and renovation
If you have bought a property that you can move into but may require some work or decoration, it is far better to move in and live in it for a little while before commencing the work. You need to see how you will live in France so you make your decisions accordingly.
If you have bought a property towards the South of France you will spend more time in the garden, and dining areas outside may become far more important than those inside.

How much nicer to arrive on holiday, or for a weekend, to a home that feels relaxed, so don't over-furnish it and make sure you leave lots of space where possible. Buy your decorations locally so that they look the part – it's like arriving at a hotel which has been decorated in the style that suits it rather than in practical dark or boring colours.

Be practical
However, that said, do be practical with your furnishings – you do not want to have to be careful all the time. If you want to have light coverings on your sofas, why not opt for some specially treated leather so that you don't have to worry about the odd glass of wine or *tarte tatin* being dropped on it! Choose your floor coverings with thought and care; tiles are used to a great extent, particularly in the southern half of France, but they can be cold. However, before you start changing things like this it is a good idea to experience them throughout all the seasons so that you can make more educated decisions. Tiles with rugs on in the winter are an excellent compromise although wood flooring can be warmer and still practical. Carpet may suit in the bedrooms but it will depend on your usage of the property, and it is easier to keep tiles and wood really clean.

Furnishing a permanent home

If this is going to be your permanent home, then it is a little different and you will want to have your own familiar bits and pieces around you to make you feel at home, but you should not try to emulate the home you have left in Britain.

It is certainly not a good idea to buy new in the UK and then pay for it to be transported to France. It will increase your costs

considerably and should there be any problems with a particular product it will make them even more difficult to sort out. So try to make things easy for yourself; there will be enough small aggravations settling into a new home without creating more potential headaches for yourself.

You have finally achieved your dream so now it's time to make your French home really look and feel like one.

Electrical equipment

Most machinery, i.e. washing machines and fridges, etc., will work in France, but moving some equipment can cause lasting damage. If you are taking your own, it is worth a try, but if you can do a deal with your purchaser in the UK to include these items, this would be a better idea. The new digital televisions will work in France but older televisions may be on the wrong system and will only function in black and white, if at all.

If you are going to buy new electrical equipment then you should most definitely buy it in France, locally. It is not only easier but essential for equipment that can go wrong that you have someone to contact for repairs, and perhaps take out a guarantee to cover it for a few years as well as getting some help in installing the machine.

Useful tips

It cannot be stressed enough that you should use the same logic and common sense when you are making decisions in France as you have done in your daily life in the UK. Here are some helpful guidelines.

▶ Don't make things more difficult than necessary; use local stores but check out the prices in two or three before making major purchases.

▶ Don't be shy about asking for discounts – they can only say 'no' and they may say 'yes'.

▶ Saving a few euros is obviously important but sometimes the service or delivery time or just ease of dealing with someone who can speak English means that you are better off paying a few euros more.

▶ Do bear in mind that if your new property is going to be used as a holiday home the machines may not get the same usage as they would in your permanent home; on the other hand, if you are going to let it out, they may get reasonably hard use without much care, so choose a machine in a price range to suit the usage.

▶ If you have bought a property in southern France, then bear in mind that your fridge may be much more important than the one you have at home. It will be filled with a selection of cold drinks, water, salads, fruit and ice cream, not to mention the chilled wine and beers that will be essential, and perhaps even some supplies that in cooler climates are left out of the fridge. Choose a fridge accordingly. An ice machine can be invaluable in some areas with particularly hot summers. Bear in mind that if it is a holiday home you may be buying easy-to-prepare food and luxury items that you would normally not have at home.

▶ Although you may not intend to spend too much time in the kitchen, you will be eating in fairly often as the food on offer is so tempting, so a dishwasher is essential if your holiday home is going to give you a holiday.

▶ If you are making the move permanently from the UK, you will probably have all the small items, such as utensils and salad bowls, that you need, but you may still find that living a different lifestyle means you have too many of some things and not enough of others. Pack carefully, remembering that you may be paying for the removal of boxes that are really of no use to you. We all collect a lot of unwanted belongings, so try to dispose of them back in the UK rather than taking them with you to France and then having to find places to put them.

▶ It is all part of the fun of owning a home in France to search out the accessories, pretty bowls, plates and ornaments that fit the character of your new home. Try to do this slowly, buying when you see something rather than going out specifically to buy it. Don't base your ideas for what you need on what you have had before – your lifestyle and daily needs will be different now.

▶ In the UK we are always trying to maximize the amount of light and sunshine in our houses, but if you live in southern France where the weather is hot for a large percentage of the year you may wish to limit it in order to keep your property cool.

▶ Your ideas on decoration may change drastically over a few weeks or months as you see what is on offer and settle into your new surroundings.

▶ If your property is not habitable and you need to get started immediately on the renovation then think very carefully about the lifestyle you intend to lead and try to place rooms correctly. For instance, it may be tempting to have a south-facing kitchen but, in fact, a north-facing kitchen will keep it and you cool in the summer months.

▶ If you are going to need some work done on your new home and have got various estimates from local artisans, do check how long these will remain valid, i.e. if you don't start the work for six months, are they likely to increase the price?

▶ You are likely to need the services of an electrician perhaps to put up your lights when you move in. Choose someone local to you; if you can get a recommendation from your vendor or agent then so much the better. Unless you are 100 per cent confident about dealing with electricity it might be best to get things done for you by the professionals to prevent any accidents – you can learn from them for the next time perhaps.

▶ You will also need to find out on which days the dustmen collect and when you are allowed to put out your dustbin as well as the rules governing recycling, etc. in your area.

must know

Shopping
Buy the essentials – kitchen equipment, sofas, beds and garden furniture – as soon as possible to make yourself feel at home, but to prevent mistakes leave as much as possible until you get to know your surroundings.

Settling in

Keeping the good will of your new neighbours and the locals in general is very important, whether you want to be accepted as a permanent fixture or are just there for weekends and holidays.

Neighbours

must know

When you visit the small shops in the village let them know that you have just bought a property there and are going to be a fixture – you will be surprised at the friendliness of all concerned.

You never know when you might need their help and you may even find that they are the type of people you would like to get to know. It is amazing how well you can converse when you speak just a little French and they speak limited English. They will smooth your way into the wider community if you have bought a property in a small village. An unannounced visit bearing a bottle of champagne will always go down well and they may even invite you in to share it – or at least take an aperitif or a coffee with them. If this is offered, don't refuse but nor should you expect to be invited into their home on your first meeting; the French often need to get to know you better before this happens, so don't be offended. Perhaps invite them over for a glass of wine the following day.

Local customs and etiquette

You will notice that there is a lot more handshaking in France – from friends and neighbours when you meet in the street, down to the local butcher and the waiter in your favourite bar. It is never wrong to offer your hand. As you get more friendly, you will find that the 'kissing etiquette' varies from area to area. It can be once on each cheek, or three pecks and, in some areas, it is four, twice on each cheek! If you are unsure as to whether you are supposed to kiss, then wait for a cheek to be offered to you.

There are many subtleties to bear in mind as well, which differ from life in the UK. For instance, never take chrysanthemums as a gift when visiting someone's house. These flowers are reserved for funerals and taking to cemeteries on *Toussaint* in November (see page 173).

Making friends

If you have bought a home on a new development, your neighbours will probably all be moving in within a few months of each other and this sometimes provides a quicker way of making friends and having a social life. You may well find that many of your fellow new owners are like-minded people of various nationalities and you will have a lot in common as you have all got similar tastes in property.

It will give you something to talk about to break the ice as you discuss how you have furnished your home and how much time you will be spending there, find out who has children and of what ages, etc. If you move in first, then remember how much you would have appreciated a friendly face and go and make their acquaintance.

Language

It cannot be stressed enough that you will get so much more enjoyment from your life in France if you can understand what people are saying to you, can watch French television and listen to the radio, and understand the news and weather forecasts, etc.

If you have not had the time or the opportunity to have lessons before your purchase then now is the time to try and put in some study to learn at least the basics of the language or even to become fluent. It is so much easier to learn when you are in France amongst French speakers all the time, sometimes having to make yourself understood and hearing the way people phrase their words.

If you are living in France permanently, you should find yourself a teacher and take some formal lessons. Force yourself to watch French television, make yourself speak in French and ask people to correct you. If you have bought your property as a second home, then either take some lessons in the UK or buy a course of French lessons that you can listen to and, again, learn and listen as much as you can when you are in France. You may never become bi-lingual but if you can gain some understanding of the language it offers so many more possibilities to you in your life in France and will make it easier and more rewarding.

Find out about the area

It is now time for you to start enjoying your French property and the area in general. It is a good idea to visit the local tourist offices, not just for your village but also some of the surrounding areas, to collect information on any events and activities that may be of interest to you.

Put away all the maps, leaflets and information you amass in a drawer in your new home, so that should you have any family or friends staying the information is always available. You can also pick up national and local train and bus timetables and contact numbers for restaurants and local taxi companies, which may come in useful as you settle in.

Local markets

The local tourist office will be able to tell you which days are market days and which towns have markets. As well as food markets you will often find that there are antique markets – ideal for those bits and pieces you need to complete the furnishing of your house – as well as book markets, although these are possibly of less interest as the books on sale will be in French, and markets for clothes and household goods.

Markets are held on regular days and are always fun to wander around, trying out new foods and buying home-made produce. If you are brave enough, you may even be able to bring home your meat in its live state – rabbits, hens and geese!

You may discover foods that you have never seen before, so try them if they are being offered or buy a small portion to taste and expand your palette – some may be an acquired taste, some you may hate and yet others may become firm favourites. However, do give yourself this opportunity of experimenting with some wonderful flavours that until now you would not have encountered.

Banks and shop opening hours

Check on the list of French bank holidays (see page 173) so that you don't get caught out, wondering why everything is closed when you had planned a shopping excursion. You will find that there will always be a *boulangerie* (bakery) open somewhere, even on bank holidays and Sundays, at least in the morning, and very often various food shops as well – as these are always a priority in France.

We have got used to Sunday shopping in the UK, but in France, in most places, the shops all close on Sundays and bank holidays. The exceptions are in the seaside resorts, which are often where many of the French go for weekends, such as Le Touquet and Paris Plage in the north, and Juan les Pins in the south.

Seasonal variations

You will be able to enjoy your local area whatever the season. Autumn and winter can be ideal for taking long walks or drives to get to know the area and surrounding regions better. This is the perfect time for long, cosy lunches in local restaurants which are not buzzing with tourists but have a loyal local clientele. A good tip is always to try to eat in the most crowded restaurant in the village.

Spring will bring a few more tourists and perhaps house owners who have been away during the winter months and, as the weather warms up, the tables outside the cafés will fill up making ideal viewing galleries to watch the world go by whilst sipping an espresso, a *citron pressé*, or a glass of *rosé*, pernod or beer.

Summer may bring the crowds of holidaymakers and tourists, depending on where you are living, but it is a nice feeling to be one of the 'natives' and to have neighbours and shopkeepers shake your hand as you pass by. As you head towards the particularly busy month of August, you may find that you prefer the privacy of your own property to get away from the crowds; however, if you are living in one of the most popular tourist areas, then you might enjoy the high life for a few weeks.

want to know more?

Take it to the next level...

▶ **Insurance** 80, 182
▶ **Utilities** 128, 142
▶ **Banks** 166
▶ **Bank holidays** 173

Other sources...

▶ **To find out about getting a telephone installed or answer any phone queries, you can ring the France Telecom helpline (English speaking) on 0800 364 775 www.francetelecom.com**
▶ **For information on the electricity system in France: www.edf.fr**
▶ **For gas in France, go to: www.gazdefrance.com**
▶ **Information about water: www.sen.fr**
▶ **Although you can get useful background information from the above utility websites, the best way to solve any queries about your personal circumstances is to contact your local office.**
▶ **For international removals: www.bar.co.uk Or you can email: sales@burkebros.co.uk info@shipit.co.uk**
▶ **If you are moving house within France, you can inform the administrative authorities on: www.changement-adresse.gouv.fr**

11 Life in France

Once you have dealt with the necessities of
modern-day living and have taken possession
of your new property and have some furniture,
utilities and a telephone organized, you can
start to relax and get acquainted with your new
neighbours. Now is the time to start enjoying
yourself and settle in to the French lifestyle
which has been your dream for such a long
time – it is the reason why you are now the
proud owner of a home in France.

Make life easy

If you have bought a home just for spending your holidays in France, then make sure that you remember that and make life easy and relaxing for yourself when you are there.

If you do not want to get in your car and drive everywhere, then a bicycle is a useful way of getting around and seeing the local towns and countryside in rural France.

In holiday mood

You can save time and effort by buying ready-made foods occasionally, eating out more often and by employing a cleaner or gardener. Pay your bills by direct debit and get them sent to your permanent home so that you can check them there – when you are not on holiday. Make sure that your priority is to do the things you want to do – unlike when you are at home in the UK and must focus on the things that you have to do!

Cars – to buy or not to buy?

If you are making your property your permanent home then, of course, you will have to buy a car. In rural France a car is really essential as there may be no local public transport, no buses and only a main railway station in one of the larger towns. To get around in your daily life, shopping, enjoying the various activities in the area, and seeing just a little more than your immediate surroundings, life may be difficult or extremely boring without your own transport.

However, if you are buying a second home, you will need to think carefully about whether you need to buy a car to keep there or just to rent one each time you visit. You need to make a rough calculation as to the time you will spend at your French home:

whether you will be using it frequently for lots of short breaks or less often for longer stays will also make a difference. Whether to buy or rent a car may depend on several factors: if you have bought in the north of France, you may be intending to drive there most of the time, and even for people further south this may be the case on longer visits.

If you know that you want or need to keep a car in France all the time, remember to add in to your calculation of the costs all the extras for the various insurances. If you are under 25 years or have family members below this age, car rental may not be an option. Set against the rental costs the costs of purchasing a car and take account of the following:

▶ If you own a car you will have maintenance and

If you live on the coast and enjoy sailing, another way to get around is to go by boat. There are many marinas and harbours for people who like messing around in boats.

insurance costs plus the responsibility of dealing with any mechanical problems on the car.

▶ If the car is garaged at your new home, you will need a taxi from and back to the airport on each visit which can cost as much as a week's car rental.

▶ You might decide to leave your car at the airport but, again, you need to add in the parking costs.

▶ Add in the interest you would receive on the money you will have to pay out to buy a car.

▶ If you intend asking family or friends to stay, you may need different sized cars for each visit and may be able to share the cost of rental with your guests.

▶ It is normally cheaper to pre-book a rental car from the UK, but as you settle down in the area you may find a local firm who can do a better deal for regular clients.

▶ Annual AA (Automobile Association) motoring cover for being abroad may be a good idea for people who will be driving to France regularly.

Opening a bank account

Bear in mind that whereas some French banks are national others are regional. Thus a bank like *Crédit Agricole*, although it has branches in almost every town in France, is split into regions, so if you have an account in the North, you will not be able to pay in cheques or cash or withdraw cash from a branch in the South or Central regions. However, if you have a credit or debit card from your bank you will be able to withdraw cash from a machine. In fact, if you have a French card you will be able to withdraw from machines at many other banks, too. Banks such as *BNP Paribas* are national and wherever you go in France you will be able to use the local branch of that bank – as you can in the UK at any of the clearing banks. This is perhaps a good reason for waiting until you know where your property will be located before you open a French bank account.

Motoring safety and security regulations

As in the UK, there are laws and regulations governing the safety and security of vehicles in France. The following is a brief guide.

Car seat belts
The seat belt laws are the same in France as in the UK; in fact, EU laws make them mandatory in the front and back of a car. Children under 12 years must be restrained with a suitable belt or seat for their size. At present, where no special child's seat is available in a vehicle, children under three years may be held by an adult in the back of a car with the adult wearing a seatbelt. Older children may wear adult seatbelts. These laws may change so be sure to keep abreast of current regulations. However, at present you can buy child seats and leave them at your French property and hold or restrain the child on the journey to and from the airport.

Mobile phones
The laws relating to these are the same as in the UK – the use of mobile telephones, unless you have a fitted in-car kit, is not allowed when you are driving and you will be stopped and fined for using them.

Drinking and driving
Drink-drive laws were slow to be enforced in France in contrast with the UK, but nowadays drink-driving is frowned upon and if you are convicted of this offence you will be fined, given points on your driving licence or even imprisoned. The police will often target certain points on a road and have the right to stop every driver and make them take a breath test, without a specific reason for stopping them and making them do so.

Speeding
Although the motorway speed limit in France is higher than in the UK – 130 kph – you will be prosecuted if you are caught speeding and for dangerous driving.

Parking fines
Even if you have a UK licence or a hire car, the authorities will still find you and fine you. UK disabled parking permits can be used and will be respected in France.

Banks in France

Regional banks are found throughout France. These are banks that you can use only for banking and withdrawing cash in the region where you have your account. Examples include: *Crédit Agricole*, *Caisse d'Epargne* (savings bank), and *Banque Populaire*.

National clearing banks you can use throughout France include: *Société Géneral*, *BNP Paribas* and *Crédit Lyonnais*. Other clearing banks with a presence in France include Barclays Bank and Deutsche Bank. You can also use Internet banking services, including *AXA Banque*, ING Direct and Egg. All cash, debit and credit cards should work in any area.

You will soon get used to the more relaxed French way of life and will join the locals in your village café, sipping an *apéritif* or *un café* and watching the world go by.

Stopping a cheque
It is more difficult to stop a cheque in France than it is in the UK. It is accepted that if you write a cheque to someone, then the money is due to them. The bank will want to know why you wish to stop a cheque and may require a letter from the person to whom it is written confirming that they are happy for this to be done. This happens occasionally when cheques are lost in the post.

Choose a bank in your local town or village – somewhere that you will be going to on a regular basis.

Bank accounts

In France, it is against the law to write a cheque for an amount that you have not got in your account. If you do this, the bank is duty-bound to honour the cheque but it will close your account and you will be prevented from opening any bank account for a period of 10 years. If you should make a mistake and write a cheque before money is in your account, phone your bank immediately, explain the problem and show them that the money is on the way, if possible, by faxing through confirmation of transfer, for instance. Or phone the person to whom you have written the cheque and ask them to hold off payment until the money reaches your account.

Moving to France permanently

As a citizen of the EU you automatically have the right to live and and work in France. Your individual status may affect the procedure but, in general, the following points will apply. Legislation is continually changing within the EU, however, so it is wise to check what applies at the time of your move.

Carte de séjour

Since November 2003 EU members may enter France to look for employment, start a business or just visit, without the requirements for a *carte de séjour*. This is the French resident permit. You may still apply for a *carte de séjour* as it acts as your French ID and it is still required for various procedures while certain institutions adapt to the new legislation. It will vary in its length or validity depending on the nature of your stay.

Bureaucracy can mean that all applications made for any reason can take a long time and require reams of paperwork so be prepared for this and don't imagine it applies only to you. It can take two to three months for your *carte de séjour* to be processed and issued by the *préfecture* of the *département* in which you live. Normally you will be required to apply in person at your local *préfecture* or *Mairie*. Applications are made individually for each family member. If you do not receive a regular salary you may need to provide proof of sufficient funds to support you and your family.

Modernizing your property

If you intend to modernize your new property but are lucky enough to have bought something habitable, it is usually a good idea to wait a few months and get the feel of the property before putting your ideas into action. Even when moving home in the UK it may be sensible to do this as mistakes are often made by people who want to make their new house too similar to their old one.

Don't make rushed decisions

In France, you may live a totally different style of life from the one you were accustomed to in the UK – hopefully, more relaxed – and perhaps spending more time at home or in the garden and having guests to stay. In these circumstances, making decisions may be better left for a few months in order for you to make more educated ones, particularly if you are considering such matters as fitting out the bathroom(s), putting in more heating or looking at the plumbing, or deciding just how much furniture to buy for each room.

Do your research

If it is just a matter of modernization, then it is always sensible to wait and see how things pan out for a few months. This will also give you time to ask a few people locally for their recommendations of local workmen and crafts people and the best place to purchase specific items – you might also be able to take advantage of sales (*soldes*) which are held at various times throughout the year.

If you are modernizing or refurbishing a holiday home, you are more likely to use it during the summer months. Get all the estimates you need and plan to do the work over the winter if possible when you will not be using the house so much.

Rule out August

Most building work stops for the month of August, so make sure you get all the agreements to start work in place and order any equipment that you want to install before August so that everything is ready for the builders to start work when they return from holiday in September.

must know

Furnishing your home
You will need to furnish your new house but try to keep it to a minimum. If you have got your whole place finished, take time to buy the little incidentals and bits and pieces that make a house a home. Exploring markets and browsing in unfamiliar shops can provide some of the most enjoyable moments of your new life in France. Take your time and just enjoy being able to wander around pretty villages or weekly markets finding those special things that transform your new property into a real home.

must know

**European
summer time**
Remember that the
clocks change in
France on the same
day as the UK but
they are always
one hour later.

Local events and activities

Soon after moving in, make sure you pay a visit to your local *Maison de Tourisme* – the tourist office – and collect as much information as possible on all the activities, tourist attractions, concerts and shows that are coming to the area – there may be many that are outdoor ones. Don't miss out through ignorance or laziness.

Festivals, carnivals and customs

Most areas have festivals or carnivals throughout the year although the summer has the most going on. There are fireworks on 14th July (*le quatorze juillet* or Bastille Day) and occasionally at other times there are carnivals for flowers, music festivals, children's festivals, the *Tour de France* and Grand Prix events, truffle and wine festivals – you name it... the French have it.

There are many customs and traditions, both national and regional, with which you will become acquainted the more time you spend in France. For example, on 1st May it is traditional to give women some Lilies of the Valley (*muguet*). In November, on *Toussaint*, every shop has chrysanthemums for sale – never buy them to give to anyone or take as a gift to a friend's home in France – they are there to be bought and taken to the cemetery only.

Christmas and Easter

Christmas Eve is much more celebrated than Christmas Day with most people eating their festive meal *en famille* on that day. Although the traditional meal may vary slightly from region to region it will often include oysters. The only bank holiday that the French take off for Christmas is Christmas Day itself. Most people go back to work as normal on 26th December and they then work right through until 1st January, which is a bank holiday. Easter Sunday and Monday are celebrated and are bank holidays, but the French do not take Good Friday as a bank holiday as we do in the UK.

Bank holidays

These are always on the day on which the date falls – so even if they fall on a weekend, the French do not get another day off work in the week to compensate for this. Some businesses *faire le pont* (make a long weekend of it) to bridge it. Thus if a holiday falls on a Thursday, they may close until the following Monday, taking Friday as a day off. May can be a particularly difficult month in which to get anything done as it is dotted with bank holidays (see below) which are made into longer holidays if people join them up.

▶ January 1: New Year's Day.
▶ Easter Monday: This varies each year. In many areas it is traditional to eat lamb – many villages have activities, *fêtes* etc. For instance, the town of Vallauris, which is known for its pottery, will have its potters out in the street offering pottery demonstrations and allowing children to make and paint their own pieces.
▶ May 1: Labour Day – it is traditional throughout France to give a small bunch or a planted pot of lily of the valley (*muguet*) to wish happiness.
▶ May 8: VE Day.
▶ May – Ascension Day. The date of this bank holiday varies each year.
▶ May – Whitsun. Again, the date varies each year.
Note: May is a month that often causes delays due to there being so many bank holidays and, depending on the dates on which they fall, this can mean that many people are taking time off work for holidays.
▶ July 14: Bastille Day – it is traditional to celebrate this public holiday with fireworks displays, and many towns will put on displays

and have town/village parties. In Paris there is always a very impressive military parade.
Note: Many towns and villages, especially those that are situated in tourist areas, will have music festivals, open-air theatre and concerts, etc. during the period between these two holidays. Aix en Provence, Juan les Pins and most resorts on the Côte d'Azur will have musical *soirées*.
▶ August 15: Assumption – there are lots of parties, music and activities in French villages. Le Touquet has a flower carnival where every float is made totally of flowers in different shapes and designs.
▶ 1 November: *Toussaint* or All Saints Day. It is traditional on this day to take some chrysanthemums to the cemetery to place on the graves of loved ones.
▶ 11 November: Armistice Day – Remembrance Day.
Note: The third Thursday in November is by tradition Beaujolais Day, the first day on which you can buy the latest vintage of Beaujolais wine (called *Beaujolais Nouveau*).
▶ 25 December: Christmas Day – the main Christmas meal, however, is normally eaten on Christmas Eve and consists of oysters, *boudin blanc* (a white sausage), truffles, champagne and Christmas chocolate logs (not fruit cake). As in the UK, families get together and spoil themselves with all the best foods. There are no other Christmas bank holidays – it is back to work on 26 December and normally a full day's work on 24 December.

French food

From market stallholders to specialist food shops, supermarkets and upmarket boutiques, you will find the staff both friendly and helpful but you need to start acting as the French do.

must know

Seasonal produce
In some areas it is hard to obtain certain unseasonal fruits and vegetables but when they are in season the taste is worth waiting for. In the bigger towns or more sophisticated areas, supermarkets are beginning to carry produce from other areas or countries so they can offer a wider range of produce throughout the year.

Adopt French customs

Always remember that you are in their country so do as the French would do. Get used to saying, '*Bonjour, Madame*' or '*Bonjour, Monsieur*' as you enter a shop or look at a market stall. Say '*Merci*' or '*Au revoir*', or both, when leaving. The French may think you rude if you walk out of a shop saying nothing. In most cases, shopkeepers are not pushy and you are not pressured into buying things – just be courteous.

Shopping in markets

You will find that not too far from you there will be at least one weekly market selling local produce – stalls piled high with colourful fresh fruit and vegetables. It is perfectly acceptable to pick up or smell the produce in order to make your choice.

Market stalls will offer everything from fruit and vegetables, cheese, bread and cakes to meat and meat products – including pâtés, sausages and salami – fish, home-made ready prepared foods, jams, honey, oils, herbs and olives. You may also be able to buy flowers or even clothes and general household items. There are often regular antiques markets which offer goods that may not be 'antique' in the true sense but which the owner no longer has a useful purpose for. They can prove to be good and economical purchases for your new home.

Market day can take over the town and offers a huge choice of the freshest produce, much of it being locally produced.

must know

Handling food

In France you won't have your hand slapped for touching the produce – it is acceptable for you to choose your produce yourself and to handle and smell it in order to make your choice. In markets or small shops, you may be concerned about which cut of meat to buy or how to cook something you would like to try. Don't hesitate to ask – you will normally be offered a recipe or suggestions for the right cut of meat to serve your purpose. Ask about foods you don't recognize; shopkeepers will be pleased to explain what they are and what they contain and may even offer you a taste if it is practical to do so.

Markets may not always be the cheapest place to buy food but remember that the produce on sale is often home grown and it is not being sold in bulk. They are also the most enjoyable way of shopping for your meals and you will know that you are buying and eating the freshest food.

Supermarkets

There are all sizes of supermarkets, from the 'corner shop' size to the big hypermarkets such as *Auchan*, *Géant* and *Carrefour*. You will probably try out a few and then make your own choices as to which you use. Many offer loyalty cards in a similar way to the UK. The food for sale in the supermarkets is fresh and often cheaper than in local shops and markets, as they buy in bulk. In some areas, the fruit and vegetables offered may be only those that are locally grown and in season in your area, and you may have to go further afield to find something out of season. The French don't import as much food as we do in the UK where we are offered produce from any country where the product is in season. Milk is not delivered and you may have to look around for a supermarket that sells fresh milk rather than longlife. Organic milk and eggs and many more products are becoming more easily available.

Specialist shops and opening times

You will still find many more individual butchers, bakers, fishmongers, *pâtissiers* (cake and pastry makers), greengrocers and wine shops than we have in the UK. You will need to check the opening times for your local area, as these may depend on whether you live in a place where people take holidays or close on certain days at weekends. However, in general, you will find that most shops do not open on Sundays or on bank holidays as we have got used to in the UK, except for the bakers who are open every day, sometimes on a rota basis with other bakers in the area so that freshly baked bread is always available. Similarly, other food shops, such as butchers and greengrocers, will probably open for a short time on Sundays.

Restaurants

We are all aware that France is famous for its food, and there is a multitude of restaurants in all the regions which will vary from the expensively sublime to the ridiculously low priced. Most restaurants in France will offer a fixed price set menu – sometimes with no choice but very often with a range of options for each course. The menu may vary from an eight-course meal to the *plat du jour* – the dish of the day. These menus will always offer you extremely good value as well as fresh food. They can also tempt you to try some dishes that you might otherwise avoid – *boudin blanc*, for instance, which is a white sausage made of chicken, or *escargots* (snails) and different sorts of offal.

Service is more often than not included in all menu prices in France; if you are unsure, then don't hesitate to ask if it is included. In bars and cafés it is usual to leave a small cash tip.

In some restaurants you will be expected to keep your knives and forks from one course to the next. Wine can be purchased by the glass or in carafes of various sizes and, of course, by the bottle as well as the half bottle. In the very best restaurants the shape and size of the glasses you are given may depend on the price and quality of the wine that you order. Always taste your wine and if you are concerned that it is not right, i.e. corked, don't hesitate to tell your waiter.

must know

Smoking
Smoking seems to be far more popular in France than it is England. Don't be offended if a cigarette is lit by someone at the next table, or indeed in an office in which you are sitting without being asked whether you mind; the French don't seem to be aware that it could upset anyone. In restaurants, you may find a clearly defined non-smoking area, although this is rare.

Buying a business

If you are considering running a business in France or buying a property with the objective of using it to produce income, then the most important things to consider at the beginning are the available budget and your level of expertise.

must know

Competition
France has 60 million visitors per year and tourism is the main industry, but this means that there is huge competition, so think carefully before you pursue your dream of opening a hotel, bed and breakfast, *gîte* complex or campsite.

Choosing a business

You must be realistic about your business projects, and although France still represents good value in comparison to the UK, it is not possible to buy a business on a shoe-string and expect it to generate sufficient income for a family to live on as well as provide accommodation for that family.

Financing for a business is available in France but you will need to check the percentage of the total that a bank is prepared to lend you to buy a business, and also bear in mind that the bank will need to be 100 per cent certain that you can run that business and pay the money back.

Tourism

Leaving aside specialist skills and services, most British people who want to earn a living in France are targeting the tourism and leisure industry, which means campsites and hotels, *chambres d'hôtes* (bed and breakfast) and *gîte* complexes.

Campsites represent the best value in terms of return on capital investment and it is also possible to manage one with no prior experience as long as you are prepared to work hard. You will need to have a minimum of £300,000 cash available and may also have to consider additional bank borrowing.

The majority of campsites for sale do not have good family accommodation, which is often a negative factor when clients are selling their home in the UK to move. A house on site will obviously increase the price of a campsite.

Hotels are best left to those people who have experience in the business, and a restaurant is essential unless the hotel is situated in the centre of a town with restaurants within walking distance. The overheads and especially the staffing are higher than in most businesses. A small family hotel of 10 to 15 rooms, which can be run with the minimum of staff, will possibly need a chef for the restaurant,

Many people buy a grand *château*, a traditional *manoir*, such as this one, or a large country house with a view to running it as a business – a hotel or *chambres d'hôte*.

whereas a large 30–50 plus room hotel will have sufficient turn-over to support staff and management.

Many people opt to run their own *chambres d'hôte* or *gîtes*, which is easier than a hotel as you do not have to provide meals (only breakfast in a *chambres d'hôte)* and involves only cleaning and a change of laundry between guests (see page 48).

Vineyards

The romantic image of crushing grapes and offering your own wine to friends can become a reality for many people. However, wine producing and marketing is not for everyone and the old saying that 'you need a large fortune to earn a small fortune from wine' is very true. The ideal estate with profit potential is a boutique vineyard of 10 or so hectares of vines with a *cave* (cellar) to make and bottle the wine, together with a limited number of comfortable *gîtes* to rent. The only way to make a profit from a vineyard is to sell the wine in bottles, direct to the consumer, and not via supermarkets and brokers. Vineyard staff and technical assistance is available anywhere in France.

Established versus new

Whatever type of business you are looking for, buying an established one with its good will, known history and potential to improve is the most economical option in the long run. Starting a business from scratch and dealing with French bureaucracy is a long and difficult process, and it will take three or more years to see any money in the till. It is far better to build on someone else's hard work! Families should bear in mind that they all need something to do on site, so as not to tread on each other's toes; the hours are long in the summer!

must know

Working in France
If you intend working in France you should check with the local *Mairie* as to whether you require any licence or training in order to carry out your trade or profession. You may be required to attend a course to prove your skills or gain a qualification.

This wonderful stone home has its own vineyard, but bear in mind that it will require hard work and expertise if you are to make good wine; expert help is always on hand.

Medical services

The E111 is the certificate that entitles you to receive any medical treatment that becomes necessary during your visit to the EEA and it is advisable to apply for one prior to visiting France.

must know

Take out insurance
If you are buying a holiday home and will only be there for part of the year you may also want to take annual holiday/medical insurance which will cover you for any illness whilst you are in France as well as baggage and cancellation insurance. Many of the private medical insurance companies offer annual holiday insurance to their members. This can work out a lot cheaper if you travel to France frequently rather than taking out cover each time you go.

What you need

You can download an application form for an E111 from the web or you can collect one from a UK post office. The European Health Insurance Card will replace the E111 by 2006. If you tick the appropriate box on the E111 application form you do not need to apply separately for this, as the details that you have provided about yourself will be used to issue you with a card automatically later in the year, prior to the expiry of your E111.

Form E111 will not cover you for free or reduced-cost treatment general medical care. To obtain this, you will need to get Form E112, which is not issued automatically but requires authorization from the Department of Health in the UK. Unless you have an E112, you will have to pay for the medical treatment you receive and you will not be able to obtain a refund of the costs.

Moving to France

Of course, if you are living in France permanently, then you will need to register within the French health system and possibly take some top-up private French health insurance, too. People who retire to France as pensioners are entitled to receive state medical services on the basis of their National Insurance contributions in the UK.

Many people who have moved to France claim that they feel fitter and healthier due to the warmer climate, more relaxed lifestyle and fresh, seasonal food.

Schools in France

The standard of free education in France is generally high, and you will have the opportunity of visiting the local available schools to make sure that they are happy to accept British children who do not speak the language.

must know

The school year
This starts normally on September 1 with a longer summer holiday than in the UK and shorter end-of-term holidays. Half terms are varied from area to area to allow children to enjoy the various facilities, e.g. ski resorts and other tourist facilities, without the whole country taking its holiday at the same time.

Learning French

It may be a good idea to get extra tuition in French for your children before you go there permanently; it is probably essential when you get there so that they can keep up with lessons in school. However, most children are very adaptable and soon make new friends and become bilingual.

Daily hours for school

▶ **Primary and nursery schools:** The schools open from 8.30-11.30 am and 1.30-4.30 pm with two hours for lunch which can be taken either at home or at school. There is no school on Wednesdays but there is school on Saturday mornings.

▶ **Secondary schools:** These schools open from 8-12 and 2-4 or 5 or 6 pm depending on the age of the child, with homework. Again, there is no school on Wednesday afternoons but there is school on Saturday mornings.

Types of schools

▶ *Ecoles publiques*: These state schools are found everywhere in France and are free. A primary school will be in close proximity while a secondary school is more likely to be found in a large town, with school buses provided. These are non-denominational schools. There are, in some large cities, schools where you will be required to pass an exam to attend.

▶ There are also secular schools – **Ecoles privés sous contrat** (under contract with the state) – which have the same educational programme as public schools, but parents have to pay part of the school fees; the other part is paid by the government. Religion can be taught.

▶ **Ecoles privés hors contrat**: The state does not give any money to these schools which are generally expensive and would include international schools.

▶ **International schools** will teach children a UK curriculum to pass the exams of the country they come from if required – for the UK they take GCSE and A-level exams. This can be useful if you move to France during the later stages of your child's education – after 13 years of age. Below this age, however, it is advisable to send your children to the local French school so that they will more quickly learn the language and make friends who live locally and generally become part of the community.

It will also help you enormously if you have children at the local school as you will meet and get to know the local families and find friends for yourself as well as your children. You will be amazed at how quickly children can become bilingual – which might be a great help to you, too, in learning to speak and understand the language.

Further education

Children leave secondary school at 16, either to work or go to a college (*lycée*) to finish their eduction, and at 17 or 18 they will achieve their *baccalauréat*, which is equivalent to A-levels but covers a much wider range of subjects. This allows students to apply for a place at university. There are no fees payable to attend university.

want to know more?

Take it to the next level...

▶ *Gîtes* and *chambres d'hôte* 47
▶ **Modernizing your property** 44, 46, 54

Other sources...

▶ **To find out more about medical services in France, either contact the French Embassy in London or look on the website: www.ambafrance-uk.org**
▶ **For information on renting a car in France, contact: www.hertz.co.uk www.avis.co.uk www.holidayautos.co.uk**
▶ **For motoring directions: www.viamichelin.com**
▶ **You can access road maps of France at: www.mappy.fr**

Glossary

Abonnement
The standing charge for supplying a utility.

Achèvement des fondations
Foundations laid for a new property.

Achèvement des travaux
Works completed on a new building.

Acte authentique
The final contract.

Acte de vente
Another term used for the final contract.

Agent immobilier
An estate agent.

Apostille
Legal stamp from Foreign Office; it is normally required if power of attorney for *acte* is signed.

Attestation
Confirmation that a transaction has taken place.

Bail
A lease.

Barème
A list of amounts, as in an agency's fees.

Bastide
Imposing stone property,
usually double-fronted, in Provence.

Bâtiments de France
Organization that checks refurbishments or building works to or near to a listed building.

Bon de visite
A form signed by the person viewing a property to confirm that they have visited it.

Bon pour achat
OK to buy.

Carte de séjour
A French residency permit and identity card.

Carte professionnelle
A licence to work within a profession that is regulated, e.g. French estate agents.

Certificat d'urbanisme
Permission for change of use of a property or outbuildings.

Chambres d'hôte
Bed and breakfast accommodation.

Château
A castle, which can be small or immense. The architectural styles vary
depending on the area and age of the building.

Clause suspensive
A condition which a contract is subject to; unless and until this is satisfied the contract is not firm or irrevocable.

Co-indivisaire
Co-owner.

Colombage
A traditional house in Normandy and parts of Aquitaine.

Commune
A small community, e.g. a town, village or parish, which is usually rural, with its own mayor and town hall.

Compromis
The first contract of reservation on a property.

Conseil Général
A regional council.

Conseil Syndical
The management committee of co-owners of the apartments within a block or complex.

Copropriétaires
The co-owners who are freeholders in a complex or block of apartments and make up a tenants' association.

Copropriété
A residence, complex or building which is split up into separate and physically distinct apartments, i.e. a block of flats or development of houses in which all the owners own a share of the freehold.

Déclaration d'intention d'aliéner
A notification sent to the *Mairie* to establish pre-emption rights.

Départements
The 95 administrative divisions in France.

Dépôt de garantie
A stage-payment deposit.

Dommage ouvrage
Buildings defects liability insurance, taken out by a developer on a building site.

Droit de pré-emption
The right to pre-empt, i.e. of the authorities to purchase a property in priority to the proposed purchaser.

Droit n'existe pas
The right to pre-empt does not exist.

Droit non exercé
Right of pre-emption not exercised.

Etat civil
Personal information provided by the buyer of a property for inclusion within the contract.

Facture
A bill, e.g. a utility bill.

Fermette
A small farmhouse in northern France.

Gaz
Butane or propane gas supplied in canisters or by tanker.

Gîte
A self-contained unit which can be rented out as a holiday let.

Hôtel de ville
The town hall – usually in a larger town.

Huissier de justice
A bailiff or court official.

Hypothèque
A mortgage.

Indivision
Tenants in common.

Leaseback purchase
The purchase of a freehold property and granting of a 9–12 year lease to a holiday company which will pay a guaranteed rental.

Longère
A long, low house, often in northern France.

Lotissement
A group of plots of land with building permission situated together and sold separately to enable purchasers to build their own houses.

Lu et approuvé
Read and approved.

Mairie
The town hall – in small towns.

Maison de maître
Double-fronted property, usually of nineteenth-century origin.

Maison de tourisme
A tourist office.

Mas
A rectangular stone property which is found in southern France, especially Provence.

Menuiserie extérieures posées
Second fixing on a new building.

Mise hors d'eau
The stage at which the roof is put on a new property.

Notaire
Legally qualified person and government representative; the only person empowered to convey property in France and collect taxes on conveyed properties. Deals with property and

family law but not litigation.

Notice descriptive
A list of materials and finishes which is always attached to a contract to purchase a new off-plan property.

Off-plan purchase
To buy a property which is not yet built from plans.

Ouverture de chantier
Start of building work.

Plan de masse
A plan of the site.

Plancher bas rez-de-chaussée
Ground floor stage.

Préfecture
The headquarters of the administration, found in the main town of each département.

Procuration
Power of attorney or proxy.

Projet d'acte
A copy of the *acte* (final contract) for purchasing an off-plan property.

Raccordement
Connection, e.g. to utilities.

Remise des clés
Handing over the keys of an off-plan property

after snagging is completed.

Société civile immobilière (SCI)
A French property holding company in whose name a property may be purchased.

Syndic
A managing agent.

Taxe foncière
Tax, as in rates, which is paid by the owner of a property.

Taxe d'habitation
Local tax payable on habitable buildings, which is paid by the person who is living permanently in the property.

TVA
French equivalent of VAT (Value Added Tax), which is charged at 19.6 per cent at the time of going to press.

Vente à terme
Off-plan.

Need to know more?

Property and legal

Agnès Crompton-Roberts
117 Erskine Hill
Hampstead Garden Suburb
London NW11 6HU
tel: 020 8455 3853
email: acr_solicitors@
yahoo.co.uk

Blake Lapthorn Linnell
Harbour Court, Compass Road
North Harbour,
Portsmouth PO6 4ST
tel: 023 9228 2759
email: philippe.piedon-
lavaux@bllaw.co.uk

FOPDAC
Federation of Overseas Property
Developers, Agents and
Consultants
First Floor
618 Newmarket Road
Cambridge
CB5 8LP
tel: 0870 3501223.
email: enquiries@fopdac.com
www.fopdac.com

Latitudes French Property
Agents
Grosvenor House
1 High Street
Edgware
Middx HA8 7TA
tel: 020 8951 51 55
email: sales@latitudes.co.uk
www.latitudes.co.uk

NAEA
National Association of Estate
Agents
21 Jury Street, Warwick CV34 4EH
tel: 01926 496 800
email: info@naea.co.uk
www.naea.co.uk

Finance

Charles Hamer Financial
Services
(mortgage brokers)
87 Park St, Thame, Oxon
tel: 01844 218956/7
email: charleshamer@
exchange.uk.com

HIFX plc
(currency brokers)
Morgan House, Madeira Walk
Windsor, Berkshire SL4 1EP
tel: 01753 859159
email: emily.stone@hifx.co.uk
www.hifx.co.uk

Magazines

French Property News
tel: 0208 543 3113
www.french-property-news.com

France Magazine
tel: 01242 216 050
www.francemag.com

Living France Magazine
tel: 01242 216 050
www.livingfrance.com

A Place in the Sun
tel: 01737 786 800
www.aplaceinthesunmag.co.uk

French Magazine
tel: 01225 786 844
www.frenchmagazine.co.uk

Homes Worldwide
tel: 01225 786 800
www.homesworldwide.co.uk

Travelling to France

Eurostar
tel: 08705 186 186
www.eurostar.com

Eurotunnel
tel: 08705 35 35 35
www.eurotunnel.com

SNCF (French Railways)
www.sncf.fr

SeaFrance
www.seafrance.com

P & O
www.poferries.com

Air France
tel: 0870 142 4343
www.airfrance.com

British Airways
tel: 0870 850 9850
www.britishairways.com

EasyJet
www.easyjet.co.uk

Ryanair
www.ryanair.com

French government agencies

French Tourist Office
178 Piccadilly
London W1J 9AL
tel : 09068 244 123
email : info.uk@franceguide.com
www.franceguide.com (French
version)
http://uk.franceguide.com/
(English version)

French Embassy
29 Old Burlington St
London W1S 3AP
tel: 020 7851 0956

French Cultural Service
23 Cromwell Road
London SW7 2JB
tel: 020 7073 1300

Taking pets abroad

Department for Environment, Food & Rural Affairs
tel: 0870 241 1710
http://www.defra.gov.uk/anima
lh/quarantine/index.htm

Weather

BBC
www.bbc.co.uk/weather

Maps

Mappy
www.mappy.fr

Michelin
www.viamichelin.com

Further reading

Books

Buying a House in France (Vacation Work Publications)
Buying Property Abroad, Jeremy Davies (Which? books)
Collins Robert Desktop French Dictionary (HarperCollins)
Collins French Phrase Book & Dictionary (HarperCollins)
Collins Need to Know? Speak French (HarperCollins)
Living & Working in France (Survival Books)

Maps

Collins Road Atlas France (HarperCollins)
Michelin France Map No.721 (Michelin Travel Publications)

Index

☾ Collins need to know?

Look out for further titles in Collins' practical and accessible need to know? series.

To order any of these titles, please telephone 0870 787 1732.
For further information on Collins books, please visit our website: www.collins.co.uk